LOWER BLOOD PRESSURE

Learn How to Overcome Hypertension with Simple Lifestyle Changes, without Medications and side Effects for a Permanent Blood Pressure Solution

Dr. Jason Mayer

Contents

CHAPTER 1- Introduction

Hypertension Overview

Hypertension, popularly referred to as high blood pressure, is a continuous condition whereby the blood flows in the vessels at a high rate. In most cases, High blood pressure does not have symptoms. When high blood pressure lasts for a longer period, there are high chances that an individual would contract diseases like stroke, heart failure, atrial fibrillation, peripheral arterial disease, vision loss, chronic kidney disease, and dementia.

Hypertension is responsible for over 50% of death cases worldwide. Millions and millions of people live with this condition in various parts of the world; some experience heart failure, acute limb ischemia, chronic claudication, angina, among others. Hypertension is also a principal causative agent for diseases like hereditary kidney disease, muscular diseases, dementias, etc.

Health experts and researchers have made several achievements as far as hypertension is concerned. More hidden information has been discovered on the causes of hypertension, the spread of hypertension, and the effective strategies to prevent and treat hypertension. However, some medical practitioners and societies are not putting such evidence into consideration. They are taking for granted recommended strategies for preventing hypertension. This is the major problem contributing to a gradual increase in hypertension cases.

High blood pressure is classifiable into two classes; primary and secondary hypertension. Some of the changeable factors promoting the possibility of hypertension include too much salt, excessive alcohol consumption, being overweight, and excessive smoking. Among grownups, one can tell that he/she has hypertension when the resting blood pressure exists in the region of 130/80 or 140/90 mmHg. Daily Ambulatory blood pressure checking provides accurate results compared to office-based blood pressure checking. Key changes one needs to make are reduction in weight, engaging in more physical activities, reduction in salt consumption, reduction in alcohol consumption, and a balanced diet. From existing research, managing blood pressure with recommended medications leads to prolonged life. Impacts of treating blood pressure to a certain range like 130/80 mmHg or 160/100 mmHg are not clear. Some studies record massive benefits, while others record zero benefits. According to WHO, about 16% and 37% of the world population have hypertension.

This book is all about hypertension. You will understand how to reduce your blood pressure using the recommended and well-researched methods. Therefore, why is hypertension discussion essential? It is because hypertension is a major cause of many common long-lasting conditions stated above-heart problems, moderate cardio, infection, stroke, and kidney disease. In most cases, hypertension leads to damage to supportive body organs, which in most cases, lead to death. It is a very critical condition if not handled in time. It will be of great importance that you know your hypertension if, in any case, you doubt your health. Always visit a physician for supervision. If you don't have one, look for one.

This book consists of three major parts; the first part comprises the factors that make your hypertension worse. Why is this important? Well, let's say you already have hypertension. If you find out which elements make your hypertension rise, then you're going to start feeling better, and you're not going to rely so much on drugs, and through this way, you will be able to prevent yourself from regression, hypertension complications such as heart disease, and many other things that you don't want to have. In the second part, there is a brief discussion of the current clinical medicine approach to hypertension. This is something that you are likely to be prescribed at a physician's office. It will describe why many of these approaches are suboptimal. There will also be a description of a more optimal treatment approaches based on cutting-edge research. Hypertension is a severe condition. Therefore, you must have a medical doctor supervising you at all times.

This program is not meant to diagnose or treat you. It is only meant to educate you and help you discover cutting edge methods to control and potentially overcome hypertension that your physician is simply not likely to be aware of. It is not because of the legal stuff; this is true. Ensure that you have a physician who supervises you at all times and if you decide to change something, then before replacing it, consult with your physician. This is absolutely and hugely important. The main reason why this is so important is that it benefits you by decreasing your blood pressure. If you are currently on the medication, this means that the physician will have to adjust the dose of the medication and this means in turn that your physician must know that you are thinking about starting a program so that he or she is fully aware of what is going on with you.

This book does not aim to make a diagnosis, offer treatment, or prevent suspicious conditions. Information in this book is only for enlightenment. Ensure you consult your doctor prior to making any step or procedure outlined in this book, more so for expectant women, or individuals with complicated medical conditions.

Epidemiology

Adults

Worldwide, hypertension is prevalent among grownups, that is around 22% of the world population. It is more prevalent in men. In 2004-2005 HBO prevalence were most elevated in Africa and lowest in the America. According to a 2016 study, Hypertension rates vary according to regions. Some regions experience high rates, while others record low rates. Rural areas in Asia such as local India settings have low hypertension percentage of about 3.4% and 6.8%. In comparison, areas in some European countries like Poland has a high hypertension record of 68.9% and 72.5%. In Africa, the rates were above average, as most countries recorded a high percentage rate of about 45%.

According to a 2004 study, in Europe, hypertension was prevalent to about 30-45% of the total population. By 2004 this had increased to 29% and further to 32% by 2017. Variances in hypertension rates depend on different factors that are still under study. There are also undisclosed continuing studies on this area and more information once the studies are out.

Children

HBP prevalence among youths and children has gradually increased in the past two decades in the United States of America. Hypertension in children, more so in those entering adolescence period, is associated mainly with some disorder than in grown-ups. Kidney disease has been considered the secondary cause of hypertension among teenagers and youths. However, in most cases, primary hypertension is experienced among many people in that category than secondary hypertension.

As opposed to Darwin's theory, where people rely on observable features with logic reasoning without illustrative support, in hypertension, researchers are still working on new ways for affordable and more accessible diagnosis, prevention, and treatment to counter the existing costly and dangerous methods. More research is always centered on what causes hypertension, ways of measuring the blood pressure, and its effects on various body organs as well as on therapies to prevent this menace.

As more data is expected from the ongoing research on hypertension, blood pressure values used to determine whether one has hypertension, around 120/80 mmHg. Hypertension requires earlier treatment to avoid future complications. Hypertension is not a big deal for teenagers. It is a big deal for adults, the elderly, young adults, and children.

Decreasing Blood Pressure

From previous research, it is clear that if you reduce blood pressure, through medications or lifestyle changes, you are most likely to reduce mortality, minimize chances of contracting stroke, heart failure, and malfunctions of essential body organs such as the kidney. Decreasing your blood pressure should, therefore, not be an option but a compulsory direction.

How then can one minimize or control high blood pressure? There exist a lot of hypertensive drugs in the market, which is sometimes lifesaving. When you feel high pressure, it is recommended that you reduce it as soon as you can. That explains why you need to have a physician for regular supervision. The major problem with drug therapy is its adverse side effects. These side effects will be discussed in the coming chapters.

There is also drug-resistant hypertension; this is where you take the drugs as prescribed by the physician and still feel the high blood pressure. Finally, the primary reason for widespread of hypertension, which many patients have no clue on, is the physicians. It is said that clinical physicians are, on average, 17 years behind the current medical research. This category includes drug therapy clinicians, non-drug therapy clinicians, and non-pharmacological therapy clinicians. Some clinicians are over 20 years behind the modern cutting edge, non-pharmacological medical research.

What is the big question? Knowing research periods is very important. This is very important; this is where most patients go wrong. They hope that when they go to see a physician, then this physician has all updated knowledge as per the current medical research. Regrettably, this is not what happens, and it's not really surprising because the physician probably cannot be up to date on the cutting-edge research on all the conditions they are handling because physicians are extremely busy attending to many patients. They, therefore, do not have time to go over the research. What does this mean to the patient? They do not fully benefit from the cutting edge medical and basic science research, which is funded by the tax they pay.

The main goal of this book is to inform you about the current essential hypertension research and especially non-pharmacological treatments that have side effects, and that can be extremely beneficial to you in your attempt to decrease your blood pressure. In the next section, there will be case studies of two individuals, an executive who didn't follow the advice of his physicians and ended up being pretty well. The other person followed the opinion of the physician blindly without checking the current research, and that person, unfortunately, ended up dying. In the following section, you will understand through the case studies how important it is for you to know the modern cutting-edge scientific research on hypertension.

Chapter 2 - Significance of Contemporary Hypertension Research

In this chapter, you will learn about 2 case studies of different people. It is a publication from the Atlantic, on an article named *"when the evidence says no, but doctors say yes."* These stories will make you fully aware of the real-life implications of many of our physicians who are not updated on the current research. From it, you will understand and think about your experiences with the medical system.

According to a review of various studies in 2015, it was realized that reinstating the content of vitamin D in blood using supplements, lowered blood pressure among people with hypertension with low vitamin D level. The studies also showed a relationship of low vitamin D with hypertension. Low levels of vitamin D is a major driver of Hypertension. Adding more vitamin D for a period of 1 year and six months in normal people with vitamin D shortage did not considerably influence blood pressure.

Case study 1

This is about an executive who was 61 years old, with excellent health. Though healthy, he had high blood pressure. He exercised every day without complaining. One day, he noticed something different. He decided to go for an after-lunch stroll on a chilly winter day, and he started feeling some pain in his chest. He sat, and the pain vanished after a short period, he couldn't believe it. This raised more questions on his mind. Young adult, HBP and high cortisol hormone, chest pain, how could that be? The following day he visited a local hospital. Doctors diagnosed him with a heart attack, and regular electrical impulses. The executive had signs of a stable angina chest pain occurring due to inadequate oxygen in the heart muscle, leading to blockage of arteries. The cardiologist recommended a coronary angiogram in which a catheter is threaded into an artery to the heart and a dye injected, which then shows up on special x-rays that looks for blockages. If the results indicated a blockage, the executives would get a stent, a mental tube that sleeps into the artery and forces it open. While resting in the hospital's desk, the executive googled from his phone, the existing research on the treatment of coronary artery disease. From the googled results, he found information from medical journals that said medications like aspirin and blood pressure-lowering drugs forms the basis of earlier treatment.

The executive was a confident and patient person; he asked for the test results. The cardiologist was unconcerned and ordered him to do more research. The executive refused to have the angiogram and decided to consult a different primary care physician who suggested a different kind of angiogram, one that did not require a catheter but instead used multiple x-rays to image arteries. That test revealed an artery that was partially blocked by a flag and so the man's heart was pumping blood regularly. That test could not prove whether the blockage had a looming negative effect. In reality, it was still terrible. His primary care doctor, like the cardiologist at the emergency room, suggested that the executive had not endured much pain. The man booked an appointment with the cardiologist. The appointment was rejected due to an irregular channel. The doctor was not going to be there, and he, therefore, opted for a different alternative.

It was at that point that he met Dr David Brown, a professor in the cardiovascular division of the Washington university school of medicine in St Louis. The executive told Brown that he felt dissatisfied by previous doctors and wanted to seek clarification. He was willing to try all manner of painless treatments. He even opted to retire from his stressful job before having a stent implanted. The executive had been brilliant to seek more information, and now by coming to Brown, he was fortunate. Brown was part of RightCare Allianz, a collaboration between healthcare professionals and community groups. The institution was very available. Brown argued that increasing medical costs without increasing patient benefits was not an excellent initiative, and that's why he opted to bring medicine back into balance, where everybody gets the treatment they need, and nobody gets the treatment they don't need.

A classic example was in late 2012 when Brown and fellow colleagues had authored a clinical publication that scrutinized each randomized clinical trial but compared its stent implantation with more traditional forms of treatment and came out with results that stents for normal patients, stop zero heart attacks and extend the lives of patients. Generally, Brown argued that everybody that has no heart attack deserves a stent. Brown added that stents, in some cases, increased cases of chest pain in some patients. Even though several steady patients receive stents yearly, one in 50 will suffer a severe complication or die as a result of how it is carried out. Brown explained to the executive that his blockage was one part of a broader, more diffused condition that would be unaffected by opening a single pipe. The cardiovascular system turns out to be more complicated than that kitchen sink. The executives started medication and improved. Several months passed by, and he still had positive health changes. Later, his cholesterol improved significantly. He had lost 15 pounds, and the chest pain never returned.

Case Study 2

In a different story, several weeks after assisting the executive, Brown and his workmates were tasked to assist on a case of a 51-year-old man from a nearby town. He had positively recovered from Hopkins lymphoma, but the radiation and six cycles of chemotherapy had led to lung pain and complications in other parts of the body. He was suffocating inside his own body. The man was transferred to Barnes Jewish hospital for a life-saving lung transplant. Upon arriving in St Louis, the surgeons could not operate him.

Earlier on, the man had been admitted to a different hospital due to difficulty in breathing. Regardless of his past history of lymphoma treatment, which can cause scarring, a cardiologist wondered whether the shortness of breath might be due to a blocked artery. As always, the cardiologists recommend that a catheter would be better. Just like many patients, he agreed to the procedure; it revealed a partial blockage of one coronary artery. Therefore, the doctors implanted a stent even though there was no clear evidence that the blockage was responsible for the man's shortness of breath, which was, in fact, caused by the lung scarring. Finally, the man was put on a standard post-implementation medication to make sure he would not develop a blood clot. But those medications made surgery potentially dangerous, putting the man at an extremely high risk of bleeding to death during the transplant. The probation had to be delayed.

Meanwhile, the man's lung tissue continued to harden and scar-like Molten lava that cools and solidifies into lava Stone. It was not until one day when he couldn't breathe in and out freely. The man had survived and went through the lymphoma stage only to die in the hospital for an unneeded stent.

The common ground from both stories is that none of the patients needed a stent. One didn't have an inquiring mind, while the other one had a smart thought. The intelligent minded individual survived. The critical issue is how an approach, rejected by current research, becomes so popular. This is the real situation that happens in real life in medical institutions. Regrettably, many certified physicians prescribe procedures, i.e., surgical procedures and other forms of treatments that are not needed.

At this point, you can tell how important cutting-edge methods are in the field of medicine. That's what is revealed by recent hypertension research.

Signs and symptoms of Hypertension

Symptoms rarely accompany hypertension, and for it to be identified, thorough screening must be performed, or by seeking consultation for an unconnected health condition. In most cases, certain individuals with HBP have reported cases of headaches, as well as lightheadedness, vertigo, tinnitus, poor eyesight, or irregular fainting. These symptoms are more similar to symptoms of associated anxiety compared to high blood pressure.

On close analysis, hypertension relates to the presence of alterations in the optic functions seen by ophthalmoscopy. The extent of hypertensive retinopathy can be categorized from category one to four; category 1 and 2 are challenging in most cases and are difficult to differentiate. Hyperthyroidism is most cases leads to weight loss with augmented appetite, higher heartbeat, protruding eyes, and tremble. Renal artery stenosis is related to a localized abdominal bruit on the right or left side of the midline, or in all positions. Aorta Coarctation often leads to a reduction in BP in rare cases in relation to the arms or delayed or absent femoral arterial pulses. Pheochromocytoma, in most cases, leads to hypertension supplemented by headache, palpitations, pale appearance, and too much sweat.

In extreme hypertension, there is no valid data on the damage of associated organs caused by an increase in BP. In such cases, generic medications are adopted in lowering Blood pressure progressively over one or two days.

In a hypertensive emergency, associated organs are damaged. Widely affected organs include the brain, kidney, heart, and lungs. The symptoms may comprise confusion, drowsiness, chest pain, and difficulty in breathing. High blood pressure during pregnancy is categorized into pre-existing hypertension, gestational hypertension, or pre-eclampsia.

Pre-eclampsia is a severe state during the final period of pregnancy and after conception associated with increased BP and the existence of protein in the urine.

In contrast, gestational hypertension is a new type of hypertension occurring at pregnancy and is majorly associated with a shortage of protein in the urine. In most cases, it is linked to hypertension in infants. In stable newborns and children, there are cases when hypertension causes headaches, unexplained irritability, exhaustion, slow growth, poor eyesight, running nose, and facial complexations, and infamous genetic variants with momentous impacts on BP. Similarly, genome-wide association studies have identified 35 genetic loci connected to BP; among the loci, 12 are new. Sentinel SNP for every new genetic locus recognized presents an association with DNA methylation at multiple nearby CpG sites. Sole variant tests from the study for the 35 sentinel SNP indicated genetic variants individually or collectively cause the prevalence of clinical phenotypes associated with HBP.

Numerous environmental factors encourage the occurrence of HBP. Too much salt feasting increases the BP among salt-sensitive individuals; shortage of exercise, too much weight can play a role in different people. The effect of other factors like caffeine intake and vitamin D shortage has not been determined. Insulin resistance, which is highly related to obesity and a constituent of syndrome X, also has a hand in the development of hypertension. Other research studies show that sugar may directly or indirectly have a role in hypertension. Salt is just a second in the channel.

Past history, for example, low birth weight, smoking during pregnancy, and shortage of breastfeeding sometimes play a role in the occurrence of adult hypertension, although circumstances associating these risks to adult hypertension are still not proved. From recent research, there is increased content of high blood urea among hypertensive people who have not been attended to as compared to individuals with normal BP, although it is not clear whether high blood urea propagates this situation or is a recipe for kidney failures. It is clear that BP could rise during winter seasons compared to the summer season. Other studies suggest that Periodontal disease also leads to HBP.

Secondary Hypertension
The cause of Secondary hypertension is not yet clear. From previous research, Kidney complications are the prevalent cause of secondary hypertension. Additional causes of secondary hypertension comprise obesity, sleep apnea, pregnancy, coarctation of the aorta, too much consumption of licorice, too much consumption of alcohol, some medicines, herbal drugs, and stimulating substances like cocaine and methamphetamine. Exposure to Arsenic on drinking water may also increase the chances of developing HBP. Downheartedness is also associated with hypertension.

According to a 2018 review, alcohol played a critical role in the promotion of high blood pressure among the males more so than in females.

Pathophysiology

Among many hypertensive individuals, too much restriction to blood flow is the major cause of HBP, even though cardiac rate does not get affected. There is proof that young prehypertensive individuals have high cardiac output, increased heartbeat, and resistance in blood flow. Such people have higher chances of developing essential hypertension after some time due to a decline in cardiac output due to age. Such hypertension mainly occurs due to fundamental thinning of arteries. A decrease in the size of capillary also plays a role too.

Researchers are still divided on whether vasoconstriction of arteries significantly promotes hypertension. Hypertension also causes diastolic dysfunction.

For older people with hypertension, there are more cases of Pulse pressure. This is an indication that systolic pressure is above the average, though diastolic pressure may be average or below average. This condition is mostly referred to as systolic hypertension. Increase in pulse rate among hypertensive grownups or isolated systolic hypertension is majorly caused by increased blockage of arterial walls, which naturally accompanies late adulthood and may be worsened when there is HBP.

Many explanations have been developed explaining the existence of hypertension. Most evidence shows the variance in how the kidneys' salt and water are handled or irregularities of gest that the SNS.

Consumption of excessive sodium and/or insufficient potassium leads to excessive intracellular sodium, which contracts a vascular smooth muscle, restricting blood flow and so increases blood pressure.

Diagnosis of hypertension

Hypertension is diagnosed based on an obstinately high resting blood pressure. The American Heart Association argues that a minimum of three resting measurements 2 times is adequate in determining the status of blood pressure. The UK National Institute for Health and Care Excellence advises that ambulatory BP evaluation is essential in confirming whether one has hypertension more in cases where the BP is approximately 140/90 mmHg.

Blood pressure measurement

To effectively determine whether one has hypertension, a good BP technique must be adopted. Defective BP measuring gadgets can always lead to wrong blood pressure measurement by up to 10 mmHg, which in most cases leads to misdiagnosis and wrong classification of hypertension. You should ensure that the BP cuff is free from air. This is exceptional to individuals with very high blood pressure readings, especially when there is poor organ function. Orthostatic hypertension occurs when BP increases continuously stand upright.

Modern Technology in Blood Pressure Measurement
Over the past period, measurement of blood pressure has been conducted with the auscultatory technique- a method brought into the field of medicine towards the end of the 19th century. Even though the method has been prone to inaccuracy because of less attention to the requirements needed for accurate measurement, technology has been used by many people for several years, even without change. It is important to note that since the introduction of this approach by Riva-Rocci and Korotkoff, there has been some visits to the moon, around Mars, the invention of more vehicles, the aeroplane and,

conception of the microchip as well as revolution in the field of agriculture, the establishment of online sites like Twitter, Facebook, Sacramento Technology among others. That's an extended period. The area of medicine has been criticized for ignoring scientific evidence and thereby adopting a specific type of measurement that is giving inconsistent results.

Nevertheless, this criticism has been covered with the publication of the recommendations of the National Institute of Clinical Excellence (NICE) in August 2011, stating that "ambulatory blood pressure measurement is recommended for regular diagnosis of hypertension in a local healthcare setting." The illustration backs the NICE recommendation that ambulatory blood pressure measurement is more effective compared to all other measurement approaches in the identification and management of individuals with cases of hypertension. The method is also less expensive compared to either conventional measurement or self-measurement of blood pressure.

Best Measurement Device
It is essential to consider a very accurate device while measuring blood pressure. Accurate blood pressure measuring devices is the cornerstone determining whether you need some care or not. If a device is inaccurate, attention to the detail of measurement has no importance whatsoever. To determine whether the blood pressure measuring device is accurate depends on the sole basis of claims from manufacturers. As a result, tools should be endorsed as per the international protocols in peer-reviewed journals. There exist multiple websites and blogs indicating exceptional assessments of all devices used to measure blood pressure. The sites provide more information on devices that have passed the tests and those that have failed the test.

Additional Investigations

After hypertension has been diagnosed, doctors should determine the major cause, potential risk factors and further symptoms, if there exist any. Secondary hypertension mostly occurs among teenagers and children, where most cases occur as a result of kidney disease. Primary or essential hypertension is prevalent among youths and grown-ups and has numerous causative factors, such as obesity and past hypertensive history. Laboratory tests are also important while trying to identify likely causes of secondary hypertension and gauge the effects of hypertension on certain body organs like the kidney, eyes, and the heart. Diabetes and high cholesterol tests are also important as they are risk factors for hypertension and other heart-related diseases. eGFR provides a good measurement of the status of kidney function- an indicator of the negative impacts of different antihypertensive drugs on kidney operations. Moreover, kidney disease can be determined through a test of urine protein. Electrocardiogram testing checks whether the heart is pressed due to HBP. It also shows whether the heart muscle is affected or whether there exist previous heart complications like a heart attack. Echocardiogram also helps to indicate whether there exists a case of heart enlargement.

For individuals above 18 years, hypertension is defined as either a systolic or a diastolic when the BP is constantly higher than the average value. Recent international hypertension guidelines have also created categories below the hypertensive range to indicate a continuum of risk with higher blood pressures in the normal range. The Seventh Report of the Joint National Committee on Prevention, Detection, Evaluation, and Treatment of High Blood Pressure published in 2003 and British Hypertension Society IV recommends optimal, normal and high normal sets to differentiate BP under 140 mmHg as systolic and 90 mmHg as diastolic. Hypertension can also be classified into different categories: JNC7 differentiates hypertension stage I, hypertension stage II, and isolated systolic hypertension. Isolated systolic hypertension is an increased systolic pressure with average diastolic pressure. It is popular among the aged.

Ambulatory Hypertension

ABPM helps identify hypotensive periods in older adults but can also be used in young patients in whom hypotension is suspected as a cause of symptoms. ABPM may also show a decrease in BP caused by intake of drugs in hypertensive patients under medication.

Ambulatory blood pressure can vary significantly in elderly patients with autonomic failure, with periods of hypotension interspersed with hypertension. As older individuals may be affected by the negative effects of antihypertensive drugs, identification of postural hypotension particularly becomes essential. In most cases, elderly patients record a decrease in BP, especially after lunch.

Fetal blood pressure

During the expectancy period, the fetal heart determines the fetal blood pressure for effective circulation between the fetus and the mother. the mother's heart plays no role. The BP in the fetal artery is about 30 mmHg at 5 months of pregnancy period and gradually increases to around 45 mmHg at 10 months.

The BP for developed infants is:

Systolic 65–95 mmHg

Diastolic 30–60 mmHg

Management

According to a 2003 study, decrease in BP by 5 mmHg lowers the passivity of stroke, heart attack, heart failure and deaths associated with circulatory diseases

Target Blood Pressure

Many experts have provided various guidelines on the lowest expected BP level for hypertensive individuals under treatment. They recommend a vale around 140–160 / 90–100 mmHg in the whole population. Cochrane reviews endorse related targets for subgroups, such as diabetics and individuals with circulatory diseases.

Many expert groups endorse a Blood pressure of 150/90 mmHg for individuals from the age of 60 to 80 years. The JNC-8 and American College of Physicians recommend the target of 150/90 mmHg for those over 60 years of age, though some experts disagree with this notion. Some researchers also recommended somewhat lower targets for diabetics, though others recommend a similar goal for everybody. In some studies, some researchers propose more rigorous BP reduction than existing guidelines.

For individuals who in one way or another have never suffered cardiovascular disease who are at a 10-year risk of cardiovascular disease of less than 10%, the 2017 American Heart Association guidelines argue that they deserve medications when the systolic BP is >140 mmHg or if the diastolic Blood pressure is >90 mmHg. According to Cochrane systematic review, there is no evidence backing the role of weight-loss diets on increased mortality, long-lasting health problems, or other complications in hypertensive people. The research indicates a decline in BP: the DASH diet, vegetarian diets, and green tea consumption.

Increasing potassium in your diet helps in lowering the possibility of hypertension. According to the 2015 Dietary Guidelines Advisory Committee, potassium falls among the nutrients that are not commonly consumed in America. Nevertheless, individuals taking certain antihypertensive medications should limit potassium intake or intake of excessive salts due to the possibility of too much potassium.

Physical exercise routines with records of reduction in BP comprise *"isometric resistance exercise, aerobic exercise, resistance exercise, and device-guided breathing."*

Introduction of stress reduction techniques are greater treatment in reduction of hypertension, but there exists no evidence where such techniques prevents occurrence of cardiovascular disease. Practicing self-assessment and setting appointments can be incorporated by various strategies to control BP, but serious evaluation needs to be done.

Importance of Ambulatory Blood Pressure Measurement

According to NICE, Ambulatory blood pressure measurement (ABPM) has been widely used over some time. It is considered crucial in the investigation, testing, and management of patients with high blood pressure cases though it has never been endorsed as a compulsory exploration. Nevertheless, according to the recent recommendation of National Centre for Clinical Excellence (NICE) in 2011, "Ambulatory Blood Pressure Measurement has been recommended unequivocally for all patients with suspected hypertension, meaning that any patient with increased cases of blood pressure record with conventional or with self-measurement of blood pressure."

The NICE recommendation is in line with scientific evidence, and the affordable cost nature of Ambulatory Blood Pressure

Measurement over conventional measurement and self-measured blood pressure. According to Gareth Beevers et al., Ambulatory Blood Pressure Measurement has the following merits;

- Multiple measurements- real BP is well arrived at through repetitive measurements.
- A profile of   BP away from the medical environment allowing identification of white coat phenomena   or masked hypertension
- Patients with white coat hypertension may be spared   blood pressure-lowering   drugs
- More cost-effective than   conventional and   individual measurement of BP.
- Demonstrates efficacy or otherwise of 24-h BP control
- Nocturnal BP may be a sensitive predictor of outcome
- Robust forecaster of cardiovascular morbidity and mortality
- Identify patterns of blood pressure behavior, such   as nocturnal hypertension
- Assessment of the effectiveness of antihypertensive drugs for the specified period

They go further to provide Requirements for obtaining a satisfactory ambulatory

blood pressure measurement as follows;

i.   10–15 min needed depending on first or follow-up recording.
ii.   The patient should be relaxed in a noiseless setting.
iii. Key in the patient details into the screen.
iv.   Choose the non-dominant arm.
v.   Select a suitable cuff.

vi.   Choose the measurement frequency- it can be at every half an hour in a day or night.

vii.   Deactivate measurement monitor.

viii.   Provide the patient with oral and written prescriptions on a material

ix.   Advise the patient to carry on normal activities.

x.   Instruct the patient on how to deactivate monitor after 25h.

xi.   Allow 25h recording to obtain a full 24h.

xii.   Day-time minimum - 20 measurements of SBP and DBP

xiii.   Night-time minimum - 7 measurements of SBP and DBP.

xiv.   If the minimum requirement is not achieved, the measurement must be retaken.

Suggested frequency for repeat ambulatory blood pressure measurement;

- Whitecoat hypertension pattern-confirm diagnosis in 3–6 months.
- Whitecoat pattern and low-risk profile– repeat ABPM every 1–2 years.
- Whitecoat hypertension pattern and high-risk profile – repeat ABPM every six months to detect the possible transition to sustained hypertension requiring treatment.

For efficient treatment;

If the low risk is controlled without target organ damage – yearly ABPM

If high risk and/or poorly controlled with target organ damage –more frequent ABPM.

Hypertension in other animals

Cats

In cats, the systolic blood pressure larger than 150 mm Hg, is considered as hypertension. Amlodipine is the immediate treatment channel adopted in this case.

Dogs

In dogs, Normal blood pressure alters according to the breeds. Generally, as opposed to cats, hypertension in dogs is determined when systolic blood pressure is greater than 160 mmHg and maybe if there is a damage in associated organs. Inhibitors of the renin-angiotensin system and calcium channel blockers are the major treatment options in this case. Other drugs are also prescribed depending on the severity of the condition.

Chapter 3- Factors Promoting your Hypertension

This chapter will discuss factors worsening your hypertension. There are several groups of these factors.

Dysfunction of the Nervous and Endocrine System.

Overactive Sympathetic Nervous System

As you will learn, one of the deepest pushers of your blood pressure is your overactive nervous system. The overactive sympathetic nervous system is a bitter fight or flight of the nervous system that helps you to deal with stressful situations in your life. It is also a sympathetic system making you relax. When you are suffering from hypertension, considering modern research, you will realize that your sympathetic system, your fight or flight nervous system is over-activated and your parasympathetic nervous system, the nervous relaxation system is also activated. Therefore, your entire physiology is in a constant state due to over-activation and stress, and through specific physiological mechanisms that you will learn about. This over-activation of the nervous system leads to the development of hypertension.

Overactive HBA Access

One thing that is close to the Overactive Sympathetic Nervous System is your overactive HBA access. Without digging around the bush, you must have heard about Cortisol Hormone. This is a stress hormone. The levels of cortisol have an impact on blood pressure. Higher levels of cortisol encourage higher blood pressure. The first two factors, overactive sympathetic nervous system, and overactive HBA access are all centered on the nervous system. This is the sympathetic, parasympathetic nervous system and your endocrine system because cortisol is an important hormone, and HBA is one of the significant parts of your endocrine system.

Insulin Resistance

Insulin is a different hormone. Insulin resistance contributes and may lead to high blood pressure. What is insulin resistance? When you consume sugars or carbohydrates, for example, pasta, bread, and other starch, you digest them, and you end up with high blood sugar levels. You, therefore, need sugar for your blood sugar, for energy, but you must also understand that too much sugar is not good.

The human body produces a hormone called insulin that moves the sugar from your blood. Insulin resistance is, therefore, a condition when many cells of your body become resistant. As a result, many cells of your body can no longer remove the sugar from your blood and transport them into the cells. Now that your cells become less and less sensitive, your body starts producing more and more insulin. Insulin over-activates your sympathetic nervous system. Through over-activation of your sympathetic nervous system, you're thereby over-activating your sympathetic nervous system. It contributes to increased blood pressure. This is why you must watch what you eat, in what quantities, and at what time.

Overweight

Being overweight is another issue. According to research from the past 15- 20 years, this condition can be described as an accumulation of fat around your organs- abdomen. Fat in the abdominal area is entirely different from fat in other areas of the body. Body-based fats track immune cells, and these immune cells start producing pro-inflammatory cytokines that ultimately have an impact on your mental health, affect the health of your blood vessels, and contribute to high blood pressure and cardiovascular disease. These four factors are essential and have a significant impact on your blood pressure.

Sleep is absolutely essential for you, not just to maintain your health, but also to control and decrease your blood pressure. When you restrict your sleep, i.e., by sleeping for less than eight or nine hours a night or having a poor quality of sleep, you are entering a danger zone. You will be acquiring a number of the different nervous systems-immune conditions, hence leading to increased blood pressure. It leads to the accumulation of tremendous stress. Such tremendous stress or any kind will still overstimulate your sympathetic nervous system that ultimately leads to hypertension.

Muscle Tension and Pain
This is a factor that most societies ignore. People ignore muscle tension and pain as long as they do not affect their daily life. People resort to swallowing painkillers. In muscle tension and pain, the more muscle tension and suffering you have, the more mediocre sleep quality you will experience. This leads to a weak immune and nervous system, thereby promoting hypertension.

Nutrition and Poor Diet
When you eat a lot of candies, much sugar, many carbs, then you are predisposing your body to insulin resistance. A poor diet can also cause oscillations-very high oscillations of concentration of insulin in your blood. As stated earlier, insulin overstimulates your sympathetic nervous system, which contributes to high blood pressure, and this is why diet is absolutely essential.

Psychological Factors
This is a reasonably surprising factor for most people. There is proper recent research that shows that people who lack purpose in life tend to have many more pro-inflammatory

markers. Meaning that their bodies are more likely to be in a state of low-grade inflammation, and this state of low-grade inflammation negatively affects the health of your blood vessels, promoting flick Blake and, ultimately, cardiovascular disease. A similar situation applies to a lack of warm and supportive relationships or feeling lonely. Feeling lonely is not bad. You may not have a family; you may not have a spouse or kids, but that doesn't matter. You can be utterly lonely; it is okay. However, it is still good to have a spouse, kids, and friends. Being alone is about something very different. Being alone is about lacking warm and compassionate and realistic relationships.

Lack of positive emotions makes your entire endocrine and nervous system be at a state of stress, thereby promoting high blood pressure. According to research, Depression is in the independence factor for high blood pressure. You need to take care of your depression or depressive thoughts on the moods that you may have in order to help you to decrease your high blood pressure.

Finally, there are poorly developed psychological skills. Human life is always stressful. That's a regular and healthy part of life you must go through. Trust is essential. The major issue is how you deal with this trust. When you have individual psychological skills, you have the opportunity to counter stress by allowing your nervous system to suppress the formation of the stress hormone- Cortisol. Lack of mental abilities, on the other hand, complicates stressful situations; it promotes different stressors, be it at your work or your home. They will penetrate your defense system, and they will cause your nervous system to go into hyperarousal and hyperactivation, hence predisposing you to high blood pressure.

Current Medical Approaches

Hypertensive Drugs

There are plenty of hypertensive drugs in the market, and these hypertensive drugs have severe adverse effects. This book aims at helping you to learn about the new methods that can help you to lower your blood pressure so that you can either ultimately go off your line to hypertensive medications or to reduce the dosage. This would be of great benefit to you. The first-line therapy for hypertension is at lifestyle interventions, and that includes weight loss, putting people who are overweight on exercise. There are research studies that show the effectiveness of these approaches to recollecting high blood pressure.

There is a difference between theoretical scientific research and how fundamental scientific research is being applied in real-world clinics. The reality of the real world clinics is that your physician often takes 10, 15, 20 minutes' maximum for analysis and consultation, and within this brief period they are supposed to explain to you why it's essential for you to lose weight, to exercise and to shift your diet. They need to describe how to change your diet. They need to give you energy and motivate you to change your life, and actually then follow up regularly to make sure that you are changing your lifestyle. In the real world, this is just not a realistic expectation that any physician can do a miracle within 15 minutes. Most patients always leave various hospitals more disappointed than how they came. Therefore, 15 minutes of talking to your physician for many people is not sufficient to change your lifestyle.

In most cases, the physicians are always behind on the current medical research, and this is why this book is published- to teach you about the cutting-edge methods that can help you to resolve your hypertension. Here is a comparison of the difference between traditional medical research and what is done at the summit clinic. In the summer clinic, people go through tones of modern medical and basic science research; you experience from the past eight years of working with a variety of conditions. There are experts in many different fields, including psychotherapy, psychology, endocrinology, who create new programs. The majority have an approach that is very different from the standard procedure, as you will learn throughout the book. People treat hypertension as a systemic sign that bodily systems become dysfunctional if clinical medicine aims to control blood pressure primarily to prevent severe cardiovascular conditions caused by hypertension.

Some clinics try to focus on the longer-term vision of trying to improve the functioning of all the body systems that cause and maintain your high blood pressure. The primary goal is to improve your health, and this is very important for you because medicine, unfortunately, doesn't pay enough attention to the improvement of quality of life. One would argue that one of the most important goals for most people is to improve the quality of their lives. You can look at treating a particular medical condition as a goal, which is one of the paths to acquiring a more excellent quality of life. One example of the difference between the way you look at things versus the standard clinician right now is the overwhelming evidence from research of how poor sleep restriction negatively affects your blood pressure.

There is a difference between sleep restriction and poor sleep. Sleep restriction is about an insufficient amount of sleep. Instead of sleeping eight to nine hours a day, you rest for like five or six hours. The extraordinary thing is that you can sleep well for eight to nine hours, but if you have poor sleep quality, you will still be suffering from the adverse effects of poor sleep. No physician will recommend you improve your sleep quality and sleep seven to nine hours to combat hypertension.

Furthermore, physicians do not influence to improve your sleep quality aside from sleeping pills. According to existing research, sleeping pills do not induce natural sleep. They suppress the functions of certain parts of your brain, and this makes you have sleep deprivation. You, therefore, take a sleeping pill, then end up losing your consciousness and results in continuous sleep deprivation.

Some clinics focus on various methods that improve your sleep. Quality is out of medications. Most physicians do not have access to this method that will enhance sleep without any drugs. Medical practitioners are still recommending people to sleep seven to nine hours. Because most Americans are sleep-restricted, they suffer from sleep deprivation. Some people wish to sleep for eight hours to benefit from the sleep, but they don't sleep for eight to nine hours because they don't have enough time and not having enough time accompanied by restricting the amount of sleep you're getting on a daily basis, puts you in danger. This is something that every single physician, based on contemporary medical research, should and must recommend to any patient. They should advise them to sleep for eight to nine hours a day. Regrettably, no physicians have a clue on this, and no physicians recommended this to their patients.

Optimal Approach

The optimal approach is a program that leads a patient to improve the functioning of major body systems. The optimal approach improves the original disorder. It also enhances the quality of life and health.

It is a reality that in most clinics, the most profound goal of any human being is to improve the quality of life. Quality life in this context means, positive emotions- when you experience being happy, this is what most people think about the quality of life.

It could be right to some extent, but not all right. Experiencing the emotion of happiness is part of quality life, but it's a reasonably insignificant part. It's about the experience. All kinds of emotions. It's about feeling comfortable and pleasant within your own body. Society today puts much attention to muscle tightness and pain, thereby preventing us from experiencing a good quality of life. It's about having a purpose in your life. It's about having authentic and warm relationships with your spouse and with your kids. It's about being whole, about not blaming yourself for things, or if you have done something wrong, then actually dealing with that thing without suppressing them or ignoring them.

You will learn that this is the most prominent concept in life, and that life is affected by, dozens and dozens of different factors. By learning to improve these factors, you can vividly increase your quality of life. Why should you be interested in quality? It is because you want to enjoy life more. There is also a shred of supportive evidence from current research, which clearly shows that improving quality of life not only enhances your medical conditions but also creates a full barrier protecting you from acquiring various disorders. Think about the quality of life as a defense wall and the medieval castle that protects you from getting sick.

The optimal approach includes improving the function of the nervous and endocrine system of regulating a person's pathetic nervous system so that you can be more relaxed. You need to understand the downregulation of the sympathetic nervous system and tranquil to save body prescriptions. Prescription, in this case, does not refer to pharmacological prescription. It's a set of procedures that creates a sense of being very calm and safe within your body. That prescription has a tremendous calming effect on your entire nervous system.

Improving sleep

It's an optimal approach for hypertension and must include a methodology that will help you to increase the quality of your sleep as well as to train you to sleep for eight to nine hours a night.

Improving your Interceptive System

Interceptive system is a system of neural receptors that measure the physiological state of your being. More information about this is discussed in the coming chapters, but it is one of the most foundational systems that most physicians know nothing about. When the system is dysfunctional, it causes dysfunction of all the systems of the nervous system, the endocrine system, and the immune system. You lose your ability to self-regulate.

Physical and Nutrition

There are lots of books out there, encouraging more exercise and a better diet. It is a fact that practice has a bare beneficial effect on hypertension, weight loss, and food prescription. What you eat, when you eat and how you eat, have a tremendous impact on your blood pressure.

Stress and Psychological System.

Certain psychological qualities, for example, catastrophizing has an impact on blood pressure. When something goes wrong, you can either deal with it or work alone with it, or you can catastrophize. Catastrophizing means that as a result of the stressful event, your endocrine and nervous systems spike in their activity, thereby leading to high blood pressure.

You need to know how to resolve depression, how to establish safe, authentic, and warm relationships with friends. Just like it is important to feel well and safe within your own body, it is the same way you learn how to create warm and authentic relationships with people. It makes you feel secure as an individual and as a group. This safety has a tremendous calming effect. Your nervous system is what you need to regulate to decrease your blood pressure. In the next chapter, you will understand how your body regulates your blood pressure. This is very important for you because once you know how your body regulates your blood pressure, you will understand what factors you need to address to decrease your high blood pressure.

Chapter 4- Factors Determining the Blood Pressure

This chapter discusses factors that determine your blood pressure. It is important to understand the physiological factors determining your blood pressure. But before that, you need to know a little bit of physiology, the essential details. This is not a small medical school by any means. Still, the information that you will learn in this chapter is crucial for you to become an informed patient or informed consumer who understands, how the drugs that you might be taking are working and how they are helping you to work on your pressure.

Consider the case of the circulation system; it is a very significant system in the body and has several major components. The first part is the heart. Its primary job is to be like a bomb. There are also the lungs, and the task of your lungs is to supply oxygen to your blood. Your cells need oxygen to function, and therefore, the way you get oxygen into your tissues and into your body is through inhaling. The oxygen goes through your lungs into the bloodstream. Oxygen from the lungs helps in oxygenating blood that goes to the whole of the body.

From the lungs, the blood goes into the heart, and then the heart pumps the blood out. Meaning that you have blood full of oxygen going into your various organs and tissues. Then you have your body; it could be muscle tissue, organs, or any part. The compartment of body cells can be divided into two sections — a section where the blood is mixed with oxygen. The oxygen is being transported from your blood vessels into your tissues and ultimately into your cells. That's how the blood loses oxygen and gradually becomes deoxygenated. That's why you have the blood coming out of the tissues in a different color. This blood is being driven back into the heart, and then from the heart, it is being transported into the lungs.

In the lungs, the blood acquires oxygen. On a closer look at the system on a higher level, it has two major components. It has a pump, which is your heart, and a bunch of blood vessels. So, you can think of this system just like a garden hose. A garden hose is an elastic bite. Once you connect the garden hose to a source of water, to a pump, which is like a heart, it will start functioning well. Inside your body, there is a heart and a bunch of blood vessels. In terms of the analogy, the garden hose has a source, which is the water pump that pumps water through the garden hose.

Blood Pressure Variables

What are the variables affecting your blood pressure? There exist two main variables that affect your blood sugar or blood pressure, the cardiac output, and the resistance of your peripheral blood vessels.

Think about an elastic balloon with a small hole through which a liquid enters and exits the balloon. Assuming that the walls of the balloon are not stretchy at all, connect a pump to this balloon and start pumping fluid into the balloon. The more liquid you pump into the blue balloon per minute, the greater the pressure is going to be applied from the liquid onto the walls of the balloon.

That's a straightforward illustration to help understand the concept under discussion. Take your time; think about it. Imagine how this happens. From the case of the liquid and balloon, you realize that the more liquid you pump, the faster you pump, the more liquid you pump per unit of time, the more pressure is applied on the walls of the vessel. If the walls of the vessel of the balloon are entirely elastic, then there is going to be an increase in pressure. The balloon is going to grow bigger and bigger. However, if the walls of the balloon are not elastic at all, so for example, they're made from metal, then the quicker you pump liquid into the balloon, the liquid is going to apply against the wall. If the elasticity of the wall of the balloon is somewhere in between, just a little bit, you're going to see the walls of the balloon. By expanding the diameter of the balloon, the pressure vanishes.

The balloon is similar to your blood vessels. The more blood your heart pumps through your blood vessels, the higher the pressure is. Two major variables can increase your blood pressure. First, if your heart starts pumping more and more blood per minute, and the second is if the resistance of your blood vessels increases, and as you will learn, a strength of your blood vessel, increases when the diameter of the blood vessels decreases.

Assuming that you are good with these two variables, try to move forward unless you do not understand the effect of these two variables on the blood pressure. Here is another explanation of how the diameter of a blood vessel affects blood pressure. Assuming you have the first, the topmost pipe and the bottom pipe, the amount of blood/water is the same, but when the canal is narrow downwards, there is an increase in pressure.

When you have blood pressure, you can increase blood pressure either by increasing the output or increasing blood vessel resistance, which means decreasing the diameter of the blood vessels. Now the question is, what increases cardiac output there? There are two major variables that you need to know. One is the struck wall volume, while the other one is the heart rate. Struck walling is the volume of blood your heart pushes into the cardiovascular system per each heartbeat. Your heart therefore squeezes, and by squeezing, it pushes out the block. This is the stroke volume. It's measured in milliliters since it measures the amount of blood your heart pumps for one beat.

Case in point, you may have a heart rate of 70 beats per minute. What happens to your cardiac output? If your heart rate is 70 beats per minute and your stroke volume is 70 milliliters per beat, then this means that your cardiac output, the amount, the volume of blood that you push through the entire system per minute is five milliliters per minutes.

The more the heart pushes out, the higher the blood pressure rate, the more frequent the heart contraction is, the higher the blood pressure. The lower the diameter of your blood vessels, the higher your blood pressure is. What therefore determines your stroke volume?

You should know that stroke volume is determined by blood volume and the contraction force of the heart. Imagine your heart contract now, the harder it contracts, the more blood it is going to squeeze for one bit. That's why the struck wall volume increases.

Another variable is blood Volume; imagine that you drink four liters of water, you add more liquid into your blood. In any system, adding blood will increase blood pressure. Taking the case of the balloon, the walls are not elastic, and when you add more liquid, more blood into the balloon, more pressure will be exerted. If the walls are flexible, then the pressure is not going to increase as much, and the walls are going to move apart, thereby increasing the diameter of the blood vessels.

There are now four variables that determine your blood pressure. It's block volume, how much blood you have in your cardiovascular system, contraction force of your heart, your heart rate, how frequently your heart beats, and the resistance of the blood vessels or the diameter of the blood vessels.

Therefore, what are the effects of blood volume? Well, several variables. It's how much liquid you add to your system. It is how much water you drink, how much fluid you drink, and then how much you lose.

You need to understand what physiological factors, what variables, determine your blood pressure. First, there are two variables: cardiac output and blocked vessel resistance. So, the more resistance you have in your blood vessels, the higher your blood pressure. In the same way, the more blood your heart pumps through your system, the higher your blood pressure is. You have also read about the factors determining your cardiac output, which are the stroke volume, which is the volume of blood that is expelled, that is pumped by your heart per each beat of your heart. And the second variable is your heart rate. Then, how frequently does your blood contract? The more frequently your heart contracts, the greater the cardiac output and the higher the blood pressure.

By now, you also know what determines the stroke volume. Stroke volume is determined by large volume and contraction force. The harder, the more powerful your heart contracts, the more blood expels from the heart, the higher your stroke volume. This means that the greater your cardiac output, the greater your blood pressure. Okay. Similarly, the greater your blood volume is, the higher the stroke volume, the greater the cardiac output, the greater the blood pressure. The blood vessel diameter also determines the resistance because of the narrower your; blocked vessels are, the more resistance they supply to the blood that flows by. In the next chapter, you are going to learn how your body regulates your blood pressure.

Factors affecting Population Blood pressure

Age

In developed countries, blood pressure increases with an increase in age, and individuals who have a higher baseline blood pressures have a faster growth compared to individuals with regular or low pressures. in rural communities in developing countries, cases of hypertension are shallow and increase in pressure according to age is minimal. A person's level of blood pressure indicates the possibility of coronary heart disease and stroke within different ages. However, in aged people, the relationship is not significant. This can be attributed to the fact that many individuals who had or are having higher blood pressure died or are dying with time, while individuals with low pressure may have subclinical or overt heart disease that makes the blood pressure decline.

Hypertension in children

Hypertension occurs in almost 1/3 of newborns; however, in most cases, there is no regular measurement of BP level of newborns. Evidence has it that Hypertension is commonly prevalent among newborns. When determining whether a newborn has high or low blood pressure, factors like gestational age, postconceptional age, and birth weight, should be put into consideration. In childhood, BP increases with increase in age. HBP should only be confirmed after thorough repetitive tests. One should however not predict that a child has hypertension before such process. According to a 2004 recommendation by the National High Blood Pressure Education Program, it is essential that children of 3 years and above have regular BP measurements per every visit in a health institution. However, the American Academy of Family Physicians side with the view of the U.S. Preventive Services Task Force that the existing indication is inadequate to gauge the level of a negative and positive influence of hypertension screening among children or teenagers showing no signs of hypertension.

Risky youths –according to Roberts Kasia, "Although high blood pressure generally affects the older populations, it's important to note that children and teenagers are at a greater risk today for both prehypertension and high blood pressure. This is because both childhood and teenage obesity rates have skyrocketed in recent years due to poor diet, lack of exercise, and various other lifestyle reasons."

Mexican American and African American children and teenagers are far more likely to have high blood pressure than Caucasian children. Remember to have all children and teenagers checked for high blood pressure.

Ethnic region

Individuals with an African background have been studied in most research conducted in North America. Still, it is not clear whether this data applies to African-Caribbean populations in the United Kingdom or indigenous people in Africa or African communities in other areas. In both studies, people with African origin staying in urban areas show a higher possibility of contacting hypertension than in the Caucasian population. Nevertheless, hypertension is not common among black people, black people living in the rural regions of Africa. It is not clear whether there is a particular standard of blood pressure, whether any specific level of blood pressure carries worse prospects for individuals with African background or whether chances of surviving are similar, compared to people with European background but with more cases of strokes and lesser cases of heart attacks. Even if obesity is corrected, the population remains exposed to socioeconomic and dietary factors and ethnic factors. Such differences may be depending on ethnic differences, and in salt sensitivity and handling. There is very minimal evidence showing people of the African population in England and America, take in more salt a day as compared to individuals of pure European background.

There is existing evidence proving that taking in more salt increases blood pressure for individuals from Africa and that encouraging salt restriction can bring more impact in life. The variances in salt sensitivity may have related to the idea that the level of plasma in renin and angiotensin in the black population is about half compared to individuals of Latin Americans and European backgrounds. Variances in renin can be attributed to ethnic differences in reaction to antihypertensive drugs.

Gender
Hypertension is not common in women who have are younger than 50. After the age of 50 years, the level of blood pressure in women steadily increases. After this age, blood pressure in women increases to almost the same level as men. As a result, the problems of hypertension are not common in women of lower ages. This evidence may be related to the fact that estrogens have favorable effects or damaging effects of androgens on the vascular system.

In a 1978 study on an individual of African origin in the UK, and a publication in the journal of human hypertension showed increased evidence of how women with a history of preeclampsia and pregnancy-induced or gestational hypertension are at a higher risk of getting hypertension and cardiovascular-related diseases in later life. Due to their higher-risk situations, such women deserve regular monitoring.

Blood pressure	Men	Women
Systolic higher than Europeans	10 of 14 studies	10 of 12 studies
Diastolic higherthan Europeans	11 of 14 studies	10 of 12 studies
Hypertension more common	8 of 10 studies	8 of 9 studies

Table 1 Blood pressure in individuals of African background living in the UK; adult review.

Source: data derived from Agyemang, C. (2003) Journal of Human Hypertension, 17,523–534.

Diseases affecting Blood pressure

In approximately 6% of individuals with hypertension, the high blood pressure is caused by existing renal or adrenal diseases. For the remaining 94%, there is no apparent cause identified. Such hypertension can be defined as 'vital' or 'main' hypertension. Essential hypertension has a connection to genetic and environmental factors, but their roles are not well known. As you would have thought, secondary hypertension is lower in primary care than in a hospital setting.

Chapter 5- Blood Pressure Regulation by the Body

In this chapter, you'll learn the body's regulation of BP. From previous chapters, you have read about factors and variables determining your blood pressure. You have read how your primary variables, your blood volume, vessels contraction force of your hearts, influence the blood pressure. The stronger your heart contracts, the more blood expels out. The greater the cardiac output is, the greater the blood pressure. A similar situation applies to your blood volume. The more blood you have in your cardiovascular system, the greater the stroke volume, the higher the cardiac output is, the greater the blood pressure. The higher your heart rate is, the greater the cardiac output. The smaller the diameter of your blood vessels, the more resistance.

Normal resting blood pressure in an adult is approximately systolic, and diastolic, abbreviated "120/80 mmHg". In the whole world, the average blood pressure, age-standardized, has remained about the same since 1975 to the present, at approx. — 127/79 mmHg in men and 122/77 mmHg in women.

Blood pressure is influenced by cardiac output, total peripheral resistance, and arterial stiffness and varies depending on the situation, emotional state, activity, and relative health/disease states. In the short term, blood pressure is regulated by baroreceptors, which act via the brain to influence the nervous and endocrine systems.

When the pressure goes up, the body tries to maintain the pressure on the same level. Therefore, when your pressure goes up, your body tries to expel more water and more sodium through your urine, and in this way, it decreases the blood volume. Considering the case of the balloon, when the blood volume is less, the stroke volume is less, the cardiac output is less, and therefore there is a reduction in blood pressure, which brings blood pressure back to normal. This is one crucial pathway through which your body decreases the pressure when the pressure increases.

The second way is the Renin-angiotensin system. The primary function of this system is to control the blocked Valium and as well as control the blood pressures through controlling the diameter of the blood vessels. Do not get scared of that explanation. When you are losing blood, your block pressure drops, thereby leading to some impact in your kidneys. Your kidneys will start producing an enzyme called Renal. This enzyme catalyzes the reaction of a compound called angiotensinogen produced by the liver.

When your blood pressure goes up, and the body starts to produce an enzyme called Renin, the Renin will convert the compound produced by the liver into angiotensin. Angiotensin means tension. This compound risk contracts, blood vessels. When the angiotensin is under the influence of another enzyme called ACE or angiotensin-converting enzyme, it is being converted into angiotensin two. And it's the angiotensin two, that acts on different portions of your physiology to regulate your blood pressure. As you consume the big Trek, your tensin activates your sympathetic nervous system. As you will learn later, the sympathetic nervous system uses the blood vessels, which increases blood pressure. It would be best if you increased the blood pressure when you lose a lot of blood.

The second thing that the Renin-angiotensin system does is that it helps the body to reabsorb water and sodium. Thirdly, it stimulates the production of aldosterone, which also helps to retain water and sodium in this way, it also increases blood volume and restores the blood pressure to normal.

Finally, there is angiotensin 2. As its name implies in terms of tension, it constricts blood vessels. When you tighten the blood vessels, you increase the resistance in the blood vessels, thereby leading to higher blood pressure. Angiotensin also affects the pituitary gland and is stimulated to produce ADH, and the ADH is worse in, retaining more water.

The result of all of these actions is straightforward, retaining water and sodium and increasing the blood volume. The explanation may appear to be very complicated. Still, the only thing you need to know is that if for some reason your pressure goes down, the angiotensin two is produced, which on the one hand, reabsorbs water and sodium or retains more water and sodium. It, therefore, prevents the kidneys from expelling water and sodium. In this way, it increases block volume and also leads to constriction of blood vessels, which also helps to increase the blood volume.

The ACE inhibitors are used to lower blood pressure. Once you inhibit the enzyme, the production of tension is reduced. And therefore, the body retains less water and sodium and does not constrict the blood vessels as much. As a result, your blood pressure is reduced. This system primarily helps you to increase the blood pressure when, for example, you're losing blood. The system is very important because dysfunction in the system can lead to hypertension. Consider the case when there is an overproduction of Renin for some reason. If you produce too much tension, there will be increased production of angiotensin 2. The more angiotensin two you have, the smaller your blood vessels are, and the more water you retain, which leads to hypertension. That's how ACE inhibitors work. They reduce the production of angiotensin two, thereby lowering your blood pressure.

How do you stimulate this system? How can you encourage the production of threads? Another pathway to simulate this system is through activation or hyperactivation of your sympathetic nervous system. When your sympathetic nervous system is over-activated, it increases the production of Brennan with the ultimate effect of you retaining more water, increasing your block volume, and that means an increase in your blood pressure. It is this effect of the sympathetic nervous system on the production of friends that are of much interest in terms of regulation of your hypertension.

There are now three variables that control your blood pressure. These are blood volume contraction, the force of the heartbeat frequency, and blood vessel diameter. Sympathetic nervous system outflow stimulates the production of Brennan leading to increased levels of rent and retention of more water, which in turn leads to higher block volume. Fundamentally, it increases stroke volume and thereby leading to increased cardiac output and, subsequently, higher blood pressure. When you over-activate your sympathetic nervous system, the smooth muscles (lumen of your blood vessel), contract and by this contraction diameter of your blood vessel is decreased. From this discussion, you realize that the effect of the increased sympathetic nervous system of flow results in greater production of Renton and, ultimately, greater blood volume. The sympathetic nervous system outflow results in a reduction of the diameter of the blood vessels resulting in greater resistance to the blood flow and, therefore, greater blood pressure.

As a reminder, your sympathetic nervous system can stimulate rent and production, leading to increased blood pressure. That angiotensin also stimulates adrenaline production, and more adrenaline increases your heart rate and increases the contraction force. While this process increases the blood pressure. A higher level of Renal occurs due to a higher sympathetic nervous system. Angiotensin two has two downstream effects. On the one hand, it constricts your blood vessels; on the other hand, it produces noradrenaline, which has two effects. Norepinephrine increases your heart rate and increases the contraction force of your heart.

The higher your heart rate is, the higher the cardiac output, and the higher the blood pressure again. You can see what tremendous importance the increase in the sympathetic nervous system outflow to your kidneys has on the regulation of your blood pressure. How does your heart contract? Well, you have a natural pacemaker, so-called SA node within your heart. It is the electrical system of your heart. There are a bunch of cells that generate electrical activity that is pressed through the entire heart and contracts the muscles of the heart.

The sympathetic and parasympathetic nerve fibers affect the SA node. No sympathetic and parasympathetic nervous system has a different effect on the SA node. The sympathetic nervous system activates the SA node and leads to increased frequency of the heart rate, which is natural because if you're in a fight or flight mode, you need more blood.

In muscles, the frequency of your heart increases, and the parasympathetic nervous system depresses the heart rate. So, there's sympathetic and parasympathetic, which have opposing effects on your heart rate. That insurance stimulates the production of adrenaline and noradrenaline. This adrenaline and noradrenaline end up in your bloodstream. And through this, they once again strengthen the constriction force of your heart.

Blood pressure oscillates every minute and displays a circadian rhythm for a period of more than 24 hours, where high readings occur in the morning when one wakes up, and the lowest readings occurring in the evening. Reduction in the average blood pressure during night times is related to an increased possibility of cardiovascular disease in the coming times, and there is an indication that the high blood pressure at night is a great illustration showing the immediate possibility of cardiovascular events as compared to daytime blood pressure. Blood pressure fluctuates over a given duration, and this fluctuation envisages negative consequences. Blood pressure also varies according to temperature, noise, emotional stress, consumption of food or liquid, dietary factors, physical activity, changes in posture, drugs, and disease. The blood pressure inconsistency and the better predictive value of ambulatory blood pressure measurements have promoted the use of ambulatory blood pressure diagnosis system as the primary method to test the existence of Hypertension.

Frequent Heartbeat and Sympathetic Outflow.

When it is increased or activated, it stimulates a higher Heart rate. Sympathetic alcohol, as discussed earlier, also affects the adrenal gland that produces adrenaline. They, in turn, also lead to increased heart rate and contraction force. All these ultimately result in higher Blood pressure. One additional very important factor is that there is now scientific evidence that all the activation of the sympathetic nervous system reduces the body's ability to get treated of water and sodium. When your pressure goes up, the body tries to maintain your blood pressure, and therefore, it expels more water and sodium into the urine. Now when your sympathetic nervous system is over-activated, this whole mechanism of controlling your blood pressure starts to malfunction. Your pressure goes up, but your body is no longer able to get treated since water and sodium are needed to bring your blood pressure down.

The random system regulates your blood volume. The more casual you have, the more retention of foreign sodium increases, which increases blood volume and, ultimately, blood pressure. Note that, the SA node regulates the heart rate. The

Sympathetic Nervous System also increases the production of adrenaline, which increases the heart rate and heart contraction. Two primary factors affect your blood pressure, the foundational factors, and this is the sympathetic outflow and parasympathetic ethical.

It essentially means that to lower your blood pressure sustainably, you need to decrease the sympathetic outflow and increase the part of sympathetic outflow. If you suppress the production of angiotensin two, there is still at the same time an increased Sympathetic outflow, you are creating a little bit of a civil war within your body. Assuming you're stressed all the time, that means that your sympathetic nervous system is upregulated. It's hyperactive. So, then you take your drug, your ace inhibitor, and you suppress the angiotensin two productions. But the thing is that you're still stressed, so your sympathetic nervous system is always going to be producing more and more. If your biological systems start adapting to the ACE inhibitor, through somewhat complicated means, and if you want to work more in-depth, it's not just about swallowing ACE inhibitors, it's about thinking how you can, in a sustainable manner, decrease the activation of the sympathetic nervous system and increase the partisan nervous system activity not just for five minutes, but for long term. You need to shift this dynamical system from one set point into a different set point.

Chapter 6- Factors Worsening Hypertension

This chapter discusses factors that are making your hypertension worse. These factors initially cause or maintain and perpetuate your hypertension.

Over-activation of Sympathetic Nervous System

There are two types of over-activation of the sympathetic nervous system. A short-term Activation that usually happens when you have some kind of a stressful event repeating in your life. There is also a second type, which is a chronic hyper-activation. These results due to many factors that can permanently shift and then maintain your sympathetic nervous system. It is a sort of chronic fight or flight state. This means that the baseline sympathetic outflow to muscles, kidney, and heart is increased, and the baseline parasympathetic outflow is reduced.

Significance of the Sympathetic and Parasympathetic Nervous system on hypertension

There exists additional evidence, clinical evidence demonstrating the importance of the sympathetic and parasympathetic NS on hypertension. A couple of quotes from recent scientific publications, like in an article dated 2010, the syndrome of neurogenesis essential hypertension accounts for roughly 50 percent of all cases of high blood pressure, essential neurogenesis hypertension is hypertension caused by overactive Nervous System. Think about it; 50 % of all cases of HBP is attributed to over-activation of the SNS. You also need to remember that while your clinical physician may recommend weight loss or exercise and change in the diet, there are other simple recommendations that you shouldn't stress so much. There is not much bad clinical medicine can do to down-regulate your nervous system. Clinical medicine tries to regulate your system through drugs. Assuming you have a stressful job, or you have conflicts at home, what is going to happen to you? You'll continue experiencing conflicts at home; you'll continue experiencing a stressful job, then you're going to come to your physician for your hypertensive drug prescription. You will be creating an internal kind of civil war inside your physiology, where you know you're experiencing more and more stress, and you're just trying to deal with this stress using hypertensive drugs. This is the road to acquiring more and more health conditions, a different kind of route.

On a much deeper level, there is a second quote from an article published in 2014. Currently, there is a consensus that the other activity of the synthetic neurosis frequently produces Pains and BP increase in essential hypersensitivity. Article from 2004 shows that over activation of the SNS is most prominent in the metabolic syndrome and hypertension connected to obesity.

By just telling the patient to change their diet and to exercise to lose weight is not sufficient. These interventions are not enough. Physicians need to use responses that sustainably lower activation of the sympathetic nervous system. This is the basis of the latest research. What is the indication for the significance of the SNS? From the perspective of science, there is compelling evidence for the significance of the SNS on your kidneys.

Role of Block Receptors

Every Adrenal gland produces adrenaline, and more adrenaline increases heart rate and attraction force of the heart, and through that, they ultimately increase the blood pressure. What then does better blockers do? Block receptors prevent adrenaline from exerting its influence on increasing heart rate and reinforcing contraction force. The pharmaceutical effects of a higher level of physiology affect the receptors. It doesn't change the ultimate baseline activity of the sympathetic and parasympathetic nervous systems. Meaning that the operation of the sympathetic nervous system is still pretty high. All it is doing is blocking the effect of the overactive sympathetic nervous system on the blood pressure. In the short term, it leads to the reduction of blood pressure, but there is a vast question of the long-term effects of these drugs, and besides, they have serious side effects.

Negative Effects of Beta-blockers
It causes nausea, diarrhea, cold extremities or any cardio hypertension heart failing, block fatigue, dizziness, hair loss, abnormal vision, negative sensations, insomnia nightmares, sexual dysfunction, Arab child dysfunction, alteration of blood cause and lipid metabolism.

Dangers of the Increased Baseline Sympathetic Outlook

Increased Sympathetic outflow to Kidneys.
This has already been discussed. It means that the sympathetic nervous system increases the production of renin, and that Contributes to increased production of angiotensin two that ultimately leads to increased blood volume as well as constriction of blood vessels.

Increased Sympathetic Nervous System Flow to Muscles
This causes muscle tightness and pain. By saying that Sympathetic nervous system activity is increased, it is not just a philosophical statement without measurements or new kind of comments that make you look nervous. It is based on quantitative recordings of the activity of the muscle fibers of the sympathetic muscle fibers. In hypertensive patients, this is how the recording is done.

There is evidence that patients with essential hypertension and even so-called high normal blood pressure. High normal blood pressure is when your blood pressure is still in the normal range but sort of on the more top end. These patients exhibit increased muscles in sympathetic nerve activity and noradrenaline release. From the sympathetic nerves, what is even more interesting is that recent research indicates that resting hyperactivation of the sympathetic nervous system can precede hypertension. This means that when you take a person who doesn't have hypertension, (normal blood pressure) and you measure the level of activity in the sympathetic nervous system over time, you will realize that they develop over the sympathetic nervous system and after that start developing hypertension which once again underlines how vital sympathetic nervous system is for regulation of your blood pressure.

Promotes Insulin Resistance and metabolic syndrome
It increases hypertension caused by organ damage. Most internal organs like kidney and other essential organs get damaged when hypertension develops due to insulin resistance. Increased baseline sympathetic outflow also predicts and increases mortality, and other cardiovascular diseases.

In the earlier discussions, there is a brief explanation of what insulin resistance is. Nobody would love to experience it. It is your body cells that usually absorb sugar from your blood; they become resistant to insulin, and that results in higher and higher levels of insulin, which once again hyper-activates your nervous system. In one epidemiological study, levels of plasma or adrenaline independently predicted weight gain, elevated insulin meaning insulin resistance during a ten year follow up period. In another study in a different region, there is clear evidence showing how innovation inhibits a fair and sympathetic activity and reduces insulin resistance. When you cut some of the nerves to the kidney, you lower the sympathetic activity and prevent the development of insulin resistance. This research shows how vital the sympathetic nervous system is for your blood pressure.

Organ Damage
This is a widespread problem in hypertension that's ultimately due to hypertension. Organs get damaged, and the higher the activation level of the Sympathetic Nervous System, the higher its level of activation, the more likely the patient is to suffer the organ damage, including heart and eyes.

Predicts Mortality.
Both mortality and cardiovascular outcomes are meaning severe conditions like my myocardial infarction. All this show activation of SNS is absolutely an essential task and ideally should be done without surgery and selling drugs since there are many side effects of drugs.

The discussion does not advise you to stop hypertensive products. As indicated, before you start taking drugs, you must be under the supervision of a qualified physician if you have hypertension. You should not also stop your eye to hypertensive medications without consulting with your physician. This is educational advice; it is not treatment. Learn to control your blood pressure without drugs, and that may mean working with your physician to learn to reduce blood pressure and gradually reduce the dosage of your hypertensive drugs.

In conclusion, what do you need to do? You need to learn how to down-regulate the sympathetic nervous system using the most preferred methods.

Chapter 7- Effects of HB access and Cortisol on Hypertension

This chapter focuses on the effects of HB access and cortisol on hypertension. It also discusses other related consequences.

Activation of HB Axis

All human beings have a hypothalamus, which produces Corticotropin-releasing hormone (CRH) that stimulates the pituitary gland that produces adrenocorticotropin hormone (ACTH). This hormone, in turn, stimulates the adrenal gland, which produces Cortisol hormone into the blood. In normal conditions, both the hypothalamus and the pituitary glands can predict whether the blood has enough cortisol content under circulation. When the cortisol level is high or low respectively, the capacity of CRH and ACTH released changes, a condition known as a negative feedback loop.

Cortisol hormone Suppresses making of both CRH and ACTH and in this way, your body and physiology manage to maintain a reasonably constant level.

Cortisol hormones are commonly known as a stress hormone because it is produced when you get stressed. Cortisol is also created when your blood sugar gets too low, and this is important to know. Those who have issues with insulin or blotch sugar oscillations, there are three main effects of dysfunctional HB access that you need to know. The first one is that cortisol's higher-level results from acute or chronic stress. It leads to blood vessel constriction, and as earlier discussed, that leads ultimately to increases in blood pressure. Secondly, chronically high levels of cortisol promote inflammation and atherosclerosis. Thirdly, it decreases your blood pressure.

You need to deal with this more psychological factor of how to acquire skills that prevent external stresses going inside of you and raising your cortisol. Here is another example, when things don't go the way you like them, you must not tend to start blaming yourself or somebody else. If you think about it, it's a combination of emotion, for example, it might be anger against yourself or anger at somebody else. You also have thoughts; for instance, you can start saying, "How did I miss that?" "How stupid of me?" all these are emotions and thoughts. You have certain inner body sensations. You might feel surgeons squeezing into your chest, the vibrations in your abdomen. This is a state of blaming a particular state of the hormones system of your endocrine system that includes the overproduction of cortisol hormone.

Think about your friends who underwent a stressful event. Perhaps they didn't like the way things rolled up. They got angry. They started thinking about and blaming themselves. They had certain sensations. The chances are that their sympathetic nervous system is an over-activated or parasympathetic system under activated.

Psychological and Analytical Skills for Stressful Situations

There exist skills that allow you to avoid stress and avoid blaming yourself or somebody else after an unexpected event. When these skills are not developed, any stressful event is likely to walk or dissolve production. You already know the stressful situations leads to blood vessel constriction and pro-inflammatory state. Unfortunately, your colleges, your universities, your schools, do not teach you these life skills and therefore you intuitively learn some of the skills from family, from parents, from friends or not learning them at all. Therefore, there are tons of people who do not have these skills. And in fact, these skills are absent to such a degree that many people could sort of seem to be attracted to stressful and complicated situations. That results in over activation of the sympathetic system. Which always leads to the resulting high blood pressure. So, this is it for this section. And in the next article, we are going to discuss the effects of depression and the lifestyle, which is so common for probably most of us.

Prolonged Effects of Blood Pressure

When blood pressure is not controlled, it can have various adverse effects that last for an extended period.

I.   Burst eye blood vessels

When eye blood vessels burst, there is a higher risk of that individual turning blind or problems with their vision.

II.   A large and weak heart

When the heart grows significant and more fragile, it is more likely to fail (heart failure). Heart failure disallows the pumping of enough blood from the heart to other parts of the body. When blood is not supplied to other parts of the body, several organs are more likely to fail due to a lack of oxygen.

III.   Aneurysms

When high blood pressure exists for more extended periods without control, it can cause aneurysms in blood vessels. An aneurysm is an enormous bubble-like bulge in the artery's wall. In most cases, aneurysms align in the main artery that brings blood from the heart to the rest of the body; in the artery that pumps blood to the brain; and the artery that carries blood to the legs, intestines, and spleen.

IV.   Tight kidney blood vessels

When the kidney blood vessels become scarce, the body is most likely to fall short of kidney failure.

V.   Heart attack and stroke

High blood pressure can make the body's arteries to be narrow, thereby limiting the blood flow. When the body fails to have enough blood, it can develop a heart attack and stroke.

VI.   Memory loss

Due to unregulated high blood pressure, a person's memory and judgment ability may be affected negatively.

To summarize, hypertension is the essential condition deserving thorough prevention, that lowers the occurrence of unavoidable deaths. Hypertension encourages the formation of many circulatory diseases such as stroke, kidney complications and many more. Nonetheless, hypertension became an independent medical concern when the cuff-based sphygmomanometer was developed. The gadget enables simple measuring of SP in a clinical setting. While using this gadget, popular signs of hypertension that can be diagnosed for further evaluation comprise fever, headache, tiredness, warm body temperature, swollen vessels, high pulse rate, change in skin complexions, change in urine color, change in appetite, poor vision, affected pattern of thinking, and sleepiness. Fullness disease can arise as a result of the high capacity of blood in the vessels.

Economic impacts of hypertension

From many healthcare centers, HBP is the most popular condition making many people to visit grassroots health centers in the US. According to The American Heart Association, the costs of HBP in 2010 was around $77 billion.

In America, ¾ of hypertensive know that they are suffering from the condition, ¾ of this group are taking anti-hypertensive drugs, but about ¼ of people are effectively controlling it. Healthcare providers encounter many challenges in their course of ensuring effective blood pressure control, such as failure by some patients to take prescribed drugs in order to achieve desired blood pressure levels. Many people also face the challenge of following the drug-taking intervals as well as making compulsory lifestyle changes. Nevertheless, it is possible to achieve average BP, and the most important thing is that reducing blood pressure minimalizes the likelihood of dying as a result of stroke and heart failure, the severe development conditions, and the expensive cost of effective treatment.

Impact of Depression and Sedentary Lifestyle on Blood Pressure

Depression

Depression and high blood pressure tend to be highly correlated, and studies show that depression is an autonomous risk factor for hypertension. In addition, you know that certain factors that because depression can as well cause hypertension.

Factors such as abdominal fat causes both depression and hypertension. Pro-inflammatory states cause both depression and hypertension. Insulin resistance and the overactive sympathetic nervous system and cortisol production are also some factors in this category. These four factors may contribute to developing depression and hypertension, which would make depression and hypertension co-exist. Or in other words, in epidemiological studies, they would be correlated. But some studies show that the relationship between depression and hypertension goes beyond correlation.

Depression can be a solo risk factor for developing hypertension, and therefore, it is essential to address depressive situations to avoid their negative impacts.

Sedentary Lifestyle

In terms of physiology, most of the science has focused on exercise physiology, which studies the effect of exercise on our physiology. But there is also a new branch of physiology that studies, sedentary physiology. What happens to your body when you are not moving a lot? Most of the people in modern times are not running a lot. First of all, there's a significant proportion of people who sit behind their desks at work, then they go to a car, they drive the car from work to home, and then they spend most of the time sitting at home. This kind of lifestyle would be considered sedentary. A substantial proportion of people also sit with computers, but in the evening, they tend to go to a gym and exercise.

What might be surprising is that the last group of people, those folks who are exercising every evening, would be considered as leading sedentary lifestyles? Well, the simple reason that they sometimes spend 10 hours a day or more sitting, even though they exercise for one or two hours a day, a much more significant chunk of time they spend sitting down, and therefore you know that your physiological processes change when you start spending much more time sitting versus walking or exercising or running. Thus, sedentary physiology would apply to these people. Now, this is one of the fundamental reasons why in your programs, you should incorporate an exercise program, but you should prescribe an hourly exercise program. It means that the person needs to stand up and do specific exercises every hour to prevent the adverse effects of a sedentary lifestyle taking place.

It is now clear that both factors have a minimal type of exercise or a more significant chunk of time sitting down and negatively affect your blood pressure. You can even exercise for one hour a day, but because 80% of the time you spend while sitting behind your computer, it will still have a negative effect on your health.

That is all for this chapter. In the next chapter, we are going to cover the standard clinical medicine approaches to managing hypertension.

Chapter 8- Standard Clinical Medicine Approach for Hypertension Control

Two primary approaches are mostly recommended for many patients. The first line of therapy for hypertension involves dietary changes, physical exercise, and weight loss. Unfortunately, up to this day, instead of these lifestyle changes, many physicians still prescribe hypertensive medications. One of the reasons is that it's much easier to prescribe medication and to explain to the patient how to take this medication rather than go into all the details about changing the diet, physical exercise and how to lose weight because these things are much harder to achieve.

History of Hypertension treatment

Chronologically, the treatment of an earlier popular condition called the "*hard pulse disease*" comprised a reduction of the blood capacity through leeches. Hippocrates highly championed the technique among others.

The first chemical developed for the management of hypertension, sodium thiocyanate, was developed in the 18th century. It had many complications thereby making it less popular. A substantial solution was developed through the development of oral agents. The initial agent was chlorothiazide, established from sulfanilamide. The compound became popular around 1957-1959. Successively, beta-blockers, calcium channel blockers, angiotensin-converting enzyme inhibitors, angiotensin receptor blockers, and renin inhibitors were generated as anti-hypertensive agents. For popularity, a hypertension agent's awareness programs were initiated in

2005. From then, every 17th, May of every year was to be celebrated as World Hypertension Day.

In the recent past, many civil society organizations, development agencies, and opinion shakers have been actively participating in the WHD. From impact records, many organizations have succeeded in driving the message home. They have impacted many lives positively. Two years later after its conception in 2005, over 47 nations participated in the program, a new record was broken yearly. For the period of WHD, many nations – in conjunction with their regional administrations, other civil societies, NGOs, and sector, promotes hypertension awareness in the masses by using social media, print and electronic media. Through the development of the internet and communication gadgets such as mobile phones and TVs, the message has reached over 240 million of the world population. Due to the annual increase in the target, many are confident that almost all the affected people will receive the information.

Medications

There are many different categories of medications jointly called. The medicines are available and are helpful in the management of hypertension.

Primary medications for the management of hypertension involves the use of thiazide-diuretics, calcium channel blockers, angiotensin-converting enzyme inhibitors, and angiotensin receptor blockers. Some studies suggest that many people record a positive impact when they use more than one drug.

Resistant hypertension

Resistant hypertension can be described as HBP that still remains high even after administration of continuous antihypertensive drugs in different approaches. By failing to adhere to the prescribed doses, one risks developing resistant hypertension. Resistant hypertension can also develop due to hereditary high processes of the ANS, a condition referred to as "neurogenic hypertension." There are existing studies on Electrical therapies influencing baroreflex as a method of reducing BP in people with resistant hypertension.

Impacts of Clinical Medicine

What are the problems with anti-hypertensive drugs? They can be instrumental and lifesaving, but they do have severe side effects, and you have read a number of these side effects, including sleep disturbances, insomnia, hair loss, and dizziness, a lot of side effects that really make your life very challenging.

The second problem is that these drugs usually in no way address the underlying costs. Hypertension, anti-hypertensive drugs aim to prevent complications of high blood pressure, such as myocardial infarction. This is a very important goal because you know from research that if you half hypertension and if you do not decrease your blood pressure, then your chances of suffering from stroke and myocardial infarction go up. It is imperative to use these drugs to lower blood pressure. But the problem is that because these drugs are not addressing the deeper causes of your hypertension, they are not meant to resolve high blood pressure. They are primarily meant to lower the blood pressure a little bit to prevent you from suffering more.

To recall what was disused earlier, the sympathetic increase in the sympathetic outflow in the processes of the SNS and decrease in the parasympathetic nervous system by half affects the generation of pathological blood pressure. What causes the sympathetic system to over-activate? Well, from earlier explanations, these are things like sleep restriction or poor quality sleep, lack of positive emotions, accumulation of abdominal fat, loneliness, stress, lack of purpose in life, poor in attrition, poorly developed psychological skills that help you to prevent conflicts and resolve conflicts, insulin resistance, muscle pain, and tension. Unfortunately, right now, the medical system does not work with most of these essential factors.

Lifestyle Changing

Another pathway for controlling blood pressure that you can be directed to do at the medical office is a lifestyle change. Therefore, lifestyle change includes a recommendation to change your diet and to exercise.

The reality of the medical office is that the physician has 10-15 minutes for each patient, most likely, the physician would see you once a month. It's tough to explain within just 15 minutes, everything the patient needs to know and to inspire the patient to act. If you think about it, it's a complicated, mind-boggling problem you have as a physician. You have only 15 minutes, and within the spirit of the time, you've somehow got to work your magic. You have to explain the dietary change, what to eat, what not to eat and not just to say what to eat and what not to eat, but to tell them why because unless you explain to the patient of why they need to do that, then most likely the appearance of the recommendation is going to be blurry. You need to tell why them why it is so important to exercise regularly.

Morally, physicians are not the people to provide proper, continuous, and regular support to ensure an appropriate lifestyle change. While implementing it, initially, you might get a little bit excited. You go to a physician, you realize, for example, you have high blood pressure, you get scared, you start to change everything. You start going to exercise, and maybe you do it for one or two or three days or a week, and then you discontinue. Once you terminate all the positive effects of dietary change and exercise, go back to zero. Research shows that if the lifestyle is as low as 31% and it's pretty clear based on modern research that it's just not sufficient and not adequate to inform the patient that they need to change something.

You need to weekly, follow up each patient, and figure out what is working and what is not working. Whether the patient is maintaining the diet, or whether they are keeping the exercise as a routine. If something is interfering with the diet, dietary change, or exercise change, maybe there's a need to adjust the diet or exercise. The physician needs to be involved regularly. Unfortunately, this is not how the medical system functions right now. Most of them are decades behind current research.

Some blogs and journals from the internet opt for losing weight to the recommended level, quitting smoking, which makes sense, a healthy diet including the so-called dash diet, which was designed for hypertension, reduces sodium, and exercise regularly. They don't say anything about sleep, nothing about stress, nothing about the over-activation of the SNS, no mention of psychological factors such as the meaning of life and authentic relationships, no emphasis on the quality of your contacts in your family. A lot of stuff is missing from internet sources. Maybe the article was not written by a physician, but a physician reviews some, and this is, unfortunately, a reality that is hard to believe. It is a sad reality that you are getting healthcare, which is, on average, 17 years behind modern medical research. Therefore, the way you acquire hypertension can involve several stages.

There are certain predisposing factors. For example, genetics, there is not much you can do about genetics. These factors may predispose you to hypertension, and then the next level factors involve precipitating factors, for example, stress, stressful environment at home, at work, or in nutrition. The fact that maybe you got used to inadequate nutrition because you grew up in a family that didn't eat well, then ultimately your hypertension goes up, before that the sympathetic nervous system is getting hyperactivated. At some point, you experience a profound feeling, and then once you realize that you have hypertension, the repatriating factors that maintain your high blood pressure kick in. And that could be, for example, anxiety. Anxiety might be scary when you realize that you have hypertension. What can you do? So many people develop anxiety after the person goes to the physician and realizes that they have hypertension. Stress leads to poor sleep.

You already know that anxiety leads to overactivation of the SNS and, ultimately, also HBP. To shift the blood pressure down in a sustainable way, you need to work with the whole variety of all of the stress precipitating factors and perpetuating factors, not just having a drug, for example, a better blocker than just block the receptors for adrenaline and noradrenaline. This is a brief-term local solution for the problems. You need to look much more in-depth and work with deeper underlying causes that are already covered. Those are the problems with the current approach to hypertension. That's all for this chapter. In the next chapter, you are going to discuss more optimal approaches to reducing blood pressure. The procedure takes into account all of the factors that have been considered so far.

Attitude

Many researchers suggest that most people generally have an optimistic attitude when it comes to disease prevention measures and more so in a high blood pressure situation. Popular attitudes helpful in the prevention of hypertension comprise of decrease of stress, a decrease of salt, reduction of alcohol consumption, and upholding required body weight achieved by regular exercise, balanced diet, and excessive smoking. According to the WHO report in 2009, suggested that pre-intervention helps in preventing the development of diseases coming as a result of too much smoking. Some of the suggestions attained were the formulation of policies targeting tobacco i.e. prohibition of smoking in public places.

Furthermore, even though the majority of people would opt to visit a health clinic on suspicion that they have Hypertension, approximately 2% of people worldwide will turn violent after the condition is diagnosed. Their attitude somewhat changes. Nevertheless, according to the WHO report of 2009, HBP is responsible for 13% of global deaths. It is also essential that nurses educate people on the impacts of high blood pressure condition on affected body organs such as the eyes, and the kidney among other organs. On top of the education, more public wakefulness on HBP killer instincts should be stressed by recommended health medical practitioners. This is due to the fact that the management of high blood pressure depends on the involvement of an individual in the treatment plan. This may comprise primarily, recommended weight, regular exercise, balanced diet, and reduction in alcohol intake as well as regular checkups and evaluations. Such lifestyle changes are critical in the management of HBP. Professor Pobee, popularly referred to as the "Father of Hypertension Prevention," in a 2007 question and answer forum, was asked the necessary action in tackling hypertension. The Professor replied that everybody must be on the move. Everyone needs to work. It must be a group activity. It calls for an individual's intrinsic motivation and deep change of mind. Physicians are just direction givers while patients are solely responsible for their health. It is therefore essential for everybody to pay keen attention to their health.

Chapter 9- Optimal Approach to Reducing Blood Pressure

In this chapter, you will learn about an optimal approach to reducing blood pressure.

Optimal Approach?

What do you mean by the term optimal approach? Is it some type of program that leads a patient to improve the functioning of major bodily systems? Not just this specific condition, a disorder that the patient came for, but an overall improvement in all the major physical systems improve their general diseases. In this case, it's hypertension. You should get a reduction in blood pressure and improve the quality of life and wellbeing. For example, you don't want to often use medications that might reduce your blood pressure, but they also, in parallel, can kill your wellbeing and quality of your life. That's why it is essential to emphasize the importance of quality life because we believe that one of the most important goals of a human being is actually to labor life. As discussed earlier, a high-quality life does not mean what is called in popular culture, happy and smiling.

Quality Life

Quality of life is a much more significant concept because it incorporates happiness, but it's much more than just pure joy and happiness. It's a purposeful life. It's a meaningful life. It's a life when you are whole when there is sort of no civil war inside your body; you're not blaming yourself all the time. It has several factors that you might learn later on. In modern medicine, physicians don't care about the quality of life. Their primary goal is to use pharmaceutical fraud to reduce the sentence or treat the disease that is bothering the patient. Much focus should be put on your quality of life. One of the applied reasons why so much emphasis should be placed in your quality of life is that because modern research demonstrates that improving quality of life improves not only many medical and psychological and psychiatric conditions but also creates a powerful barrier protecting you from acquiring new disorders.

Factors Determining Quality Life

Six significant factors can broadly describe your state of health. These are intellectual wellbeing, emotional wellbeing, social wellbeing, physiological wellbeing, physical wellbeing, and psychological wellbeing. An optimal intervention should positively affect all these factors. You may ask why? Well, for a simple explanation, here is an example, consider the term "emotional" it is lack of experiencing positive, pleasant emotions, and it contributes to hypertension. Naturally, you would want to balance out and to normalize your emotional wellbeing. For social welfare, as discussed earlier, you may have a spouse or a family, but maybe your relationship is not very warm, authentic, and supportive. By improving that relationship, you can lower your blood pressure. Social wellbeing, therefore, has a tremendous contribution to your overall physiological health, psychological health, and blood pressure.

Furthermore, social wellbeing is much more than just purely having warm, authentic relationships. It describes more broadly your relationship with the community and society at large. Do you feel that you are part of the community? Did you think that you may have a contribution to the community? All these factors discussed by sociologists are significant for your health, not physiological wellbeing.

Physiology- Internal Conflicts

Physiology theatrically affects people. It is more about, for example, muscle pain, muscle tension. Earlier discussions have indicated how muscle pain and anxiety, overstimulate your sympathetic nervous system, and it also decreases the quality of your sleep. All of these reduce the quality of sleep, and the over-exercise sympathetic nervous system contributes to high blood pressure and psychological wellbeing.

Many factors cause internal conflict; from earlier discussions, there is self-blame or blaming others. In terms of self-blame, what that means is that you experience an internal civil war where one part of yourself plains another part of yourself. When you ignore your emotions, be they positive or negative, you may be doing a disservice to yourself. These are examples of sort of a civil war going on inside of your body. This immediately has an impact on the activity of your sympathetic nervous system and HB axis, of course, as well as intellectual wellbeing. This is more about being good at trying to establish cause and effect relationships and knowing when these cause and effects relationships are valid and versus when they're just something that comes out of your imagination.

For example, when you have a conflict, you are treating this conflict by something that you or another person did or set. Now if you look one level deeper, you may notice that you tend to get into disagreements because for example, you were sleep-deprived, you were tired, you were exhausted, and it's not something that the other person has caused on you, but it's your sub-optimal physiological state of being. This is just an example when it's effortless to jump to a wrong conclusion and make one cause and effect statement once we make the wrong cause and statement that ultimately leads us to a stressful situation. These situations activate the sympathetic system and depress the parasympathetic system. This is why it is imperative to work with all of the base six factors.

Chapter 10- Hypertension Program

This chapter talks about the hypertension program. Four major deeper factors cause or define hypertension; for example, it has been discussed that chronic sympathetic nervous system over-activation and depression leads to hypertension. Your question is that how do you shift nervous system activity to a healthier level? Four factors cause hypertension on a deeper level.

Dysfunctional Interception is one of them. It primarily causes dysfunction and several different systems of the body that are either emotional or psychological. This is one of the reasons why it is so hugely important. Poor nutrition, inappropriate lifestyle, and lack of exercise, and then social and psychological dysfunction also comprise the factors that profoundly cause hypertension. These are things like loneliness, lack of purpose in life, feeling guilty, and so on.

When you work with people with hypertension, you take people longitudinally and sequentially through certain stages.

Healing the Interoceptive System

Stage one is always focused on the interoceptive system. First, what is interception? You have neural receptors that register the physiological state of your body, and these receptors spread out literally through your entire body. Information from these receptors goes up through your spinal cord, into your brain for processing and to the interoceptive system. You can feel physical and emotional sensations. For example, pain, sadness, warmness, happiness. This is the system that makes us alive. Because if for a second you had mentioned that you feel no pain, no warmth, no sadness, no happiness, you feel nothing.

Well, this is what happens if you were to cut out the interoceptive system, you will just not feel anything. The brain uses data it acquires from the interceptor to self-regulate, and therefore when the interoceptive system is not working, your entire physiology gradually gets out of water. It's not just your physiology; it's your psychological wellbeing; it's your emotional wellbeing. An excellent example to understand what interoceptive system a car is. Imagine that your car suddenly breaks down and you start thinking that one maybe it's the electric system. Something may be wrong with the electricity, or perhaps the engine dies, and then you take it to the mechanic, and the mechanic does not know. Maybe in the process, you start thinking that you ran out of fuel. Upon looking at the panel, you notice that you have enough fuel. You start thinking that it could be an electrical problem again. Finally, you figure out things to a mechanic. Yeah, you ran out of gas.

This is an example of how internal sensors of any kind of system are vital. Nowadays, full electronic sensors, that sense all kinds of stuff, are crucial to cars to operate. If these sensors break down, the car loses the ability to regulate the internal processes, and the same thing happens with your body. If your interoceptive system becomes dysfunctional, it becomes much harder to tell regularly.

When you get tired, you're no longer at rest. When you are hungry, you no longer go and acquire some food and feed yourself. When you're thirsty, you are not drinking water. When you become sad, you don't realize that you become unhappy. When you are happy, you don't even know if you're happy. Your ability to sense what is going on inside you calms down very fast. Your endocrine system ends up having problems. You start experiencing sleep issues. If you don't know when you're hungry, your body will not get the nutrients it needs; all these examples may sound strange. It happens to a lot of people under the influence of either chronic stress or traumatic stress.

It mostly happens to veterans, but you don't need to go to war to start experiencing problems. Many people are under somewhat chronic high levels of trust, and one of the first things that trust does to you is that it gradually kills your interest after the system. When your interoceptive system is not functioning well, you start having conflicts with your spouses, your friends and your colleagues at work because you cannot feel what is going on with you and what is going on with another person. Other examples of the importance of dysfunction of interoceptive systems can involve pain and muscle tension. The dysfunction of the interoceptive system can also cause pain and muscle tension. Depression and anxiety are interoceptive related disorders in depression many people are complaining about not feeling anything.

Many physicians have admitted that whenever they started teaching people to create pleasant sensations, then within their body, depression gradually declines. Based on the experience working with veterans, many health practitioners argued that they developed traumatic stress symptoms when they learn to use interest sets of a system to control their psychological and emotional state of being. Often, it's not even about feeling pleasant sensations; it's just about being feeling any feelings. When the person is depressed, and manages to create some sort of sensations, then that could be anxiety. Often anxieties are associated with several strange sensations. When you teach the person to actually regulate the feelings, the stress starts stepping away.

To recap, dysfunctional interception underlies almost all the factors that contribute to overstimulating the sympathetic nervous system and the HPA axis. It leads to poor sleep and a lack of positive emotions. It causes problems in your senses.

You will not feel much inside, and you will start craving for more food. This is because when you eat, you supply, at least some sort of sensations through your tongue, and it makes you feel alive. The feeling you get inside your body, the more you want to have some kind of external factor for stimulation. It could be stimulation through movies; it could be stimulation through eating. Depression is also very much connected to interoceptive and dysfunction, muscle pain intention, and lack of purpose in life. You can create the foundational purpose in life by helping your physiological system to feel well when you learn, and that's part of the problem when you learn to satisfy on every deep level the needs of your physiology that immediately creates meaning and purpose in life. That's a foundation of the meaning and purpose of life. On top of that foundation, you can build up more higher-level meanings and purposes like achieving goals like education, marrying, having kids, and so on. But when you don't have that foundational level of purpose and meaning on higher levels, you end up being very unstable since you end up being like a house without a foundation.

When the system intracept becomes dysfunctional, you are much more likely to suffer more stress and cause over-activation of the sympathetic nervous system. So, all of the factors that ultimately contribute to an overstimulated sympathetic nervous system are essential in rearising your high blood pressure. All these factors aren't impacted by dysfunctional intraception, and therefore it is critical to stabilizing the interoceptive system first.

Are you going to hear about intraception from your physician? Fortunately, many physicians most likely, do not even know what interoceptive system is nowadays. You will find plenty of research papers connecting intraception to different disorders.

Restoring the Interoceptive System

To restore the interoceptive system, there are several programs or prescriptions. Prescriptions in this context do not mean the actual order of medications. These are non-pharmacological prescriptions.

Ocean of Inner Body Sensations.
You need to learn each spot of your body to feel the sensations that leave in this spot. This is the foundation. It doesn't matter whether these sensations are pleasant or unpleasant. It's just a matter of sensing these sensations because physiologically, it is the significant sensations that come from each point in a tiny part of your brain and create your sensory self. This is made possible through independent sensory ability. Unless you have a stable sense of existence, it's sort of meaningless to work in higher-level functions of your body as a first step. You just need to maximize your physiology to feel that you exist.

Behavior change
If in the first step, you learn to sense each spot of your body. In the second one, you learn to change your behavior. You create pleasant and comfortable sensations at each spot of your body. As soon as you learn to do that, your nervous system literally calms down.

The sympathetic nervous system reduces its activation. It would be best if you learned to identify unpleasant sensations. This is simply because frequently when people feel uncomfortable feelings, they start getting anxious and nervous, and that overstimulates the nervous system. Each step will be discussed separately. While discussing the ocean of inner body sensations, that leads to the downregulation of sympathetic nervous system, improving sleep and reducing depression and anxiety, it was mentioned that the most powerful effect is that it creates a very fundamental sense of existence, which is required to build up the higher-level functions. Now, the tranquil and safe body also down-regulates the sympathetic nervous system and level of cortisol. It improves your sleep, depression, and anxiety, learning to bear with an unpleasant sensation. It will help you to avoid catastrophizing. When something goes wrong, you start catastrophizing. These are emotions, thoughts that ultimately cause even more sensations. The more pleasant feelings you have, the more views you have, finally, this may end up in a panic attack.

Soft tissue House

Once you are in touch with your bodies' sensations and know how to create pleasant feelings, you are ready to start healing your soft tissues. Soft tissue house is of utmost importance for the health of your nervous system. Why? Your nervous system and muscle tissue are a lot like fish living in a Lake. The fish is like the nervous system, and the lake is like your muscle tissue. Even in the Lake, when the water is clean, the fish is healthy. When water gets contaminated, the fish gets sick. Something similar goes for the nervous system. The nervous system lives in muscle tissue. They are new rule receptors, which are embedded in muscle and connective tissue. When muscle tissue is healthy and pain-free, the nervous system is healthy. On the other hand, when muscle tissue is tight and painful, the nervous system gets overactive. This is very important to understand because when the nervous system is being discussed, you can think of the nervous system as, for example, your brain, and then there are new rule receptors that are spread out through your entire body.

When the muscle tissue is hard and unhealthy, the nervous system believes in an unhealthy environment. You know the importance of the situation. Assuming you have a kid, who grew up around chemical plants and these artificial plants produce and speed out chemicals into the atmosphere. In most instances, a kid may acquire asthma, and it would be understandable that asthma might be related to the chemical contamination of the air when breathed in. The kid may go to the physician, and the physician may prescribe him an inhaler, that's a very medical approach. Another approach is that maybe he still needs an inhaler for a little bit, but he needs to change the environment. He needs to move to the mountains, where the air will be of a good quality hence better feeling. The child may still need the inhaler for a little bit, but it's likely that at least the progression of his disorder will slow down by breathing fresh air.

This example emphasizes the importance of changing the environment within which you operate. It applies not only to the importance of healing the soft tissues to make your nervous system healthy but also about your social environment. When you start changing, you might have noticed in your life that when you change the social environment, when you change the kind of people that you are friends with and associate with, then you are changed as well. This is not a suggestion that you should improve your social environment. This is just an example to demonstrate that soft tissues are very profound in your health. One of the ways they're essential is the different ways they hold to heal your interoceptive system. They release pain intention in your body.

Sensory Based Depression Prescription

If you think about it, depression is simply a label. The word depression is just a label. Labels are hazardous. The reason why they are very dangerous is that people ignore that names are created from different components. If you know elements, you can work with each element. But if you don't know the parts creating that label, then you will be stacked with the name and will not do anything about the label. For instance, the tag of depression is composed of several components. It's a particular state of your endocrine system. These are specified in the body sensation. You may be feeling tired. That could be due to a specific mood, emotions, and particular thoughts. One of the keys to resolving depression is changing one component at a time. For example, you can focus on body sensations. When dealing with people with depressive moods or depression too, they change their impressions. Often, they complain over feeling black hole or nothingness insight. When they start feeling the sensations and a pleasant sensation within their body, then this component is removed.

In that case, the inner body sensations are normal and stabilized. Then you can start working with the emotions and their thoughts. Ask yourself where the difference originates, what creates a label, what components you can work, and at what rate?

Foundation of depression is either body sensations in the state of the endocrine system meaning depressive patients feel a depressive black hole inside. And this is resolved with a tranquil body prescription that is discussed in the earlier chapters.

Now, once intraception no longer contributes to depression, you can work with emotions, moods, and cognitive skills. That's how people are very different. For example, from psychotherapy or psychologist, if a depressive patient goes to a psychotherapist or psychologist, they're going to start talking about how they feel, what emotions they experience, what kind of conversations they have with their family. Why they act in a certain way. You don't want to touch any psychology or emotions whatsoever as long as the client's interceptive system is dysfunctional because you know that as long as the interoceptive system is dysfunctional, feelings are unbalanced, his emotions are in violence, and his many psychological functions are unstable.

What's the point of talking when you know that the foundation is not working? To help you understand this analogy, imagine a house, and the house is going in a specific direction. Now that you see the house going in a particular direction is because of the foundation. So, it would be best if you worked with the foundation, but the other option is to work yourself. You can see that the roof went in a given direction, and then you start telling yourself that you are God, and you correct the rule. You don't need to adjust a little. You need to work with the foundational skills. As soon as you alter the foundational skills, the higher-level skills normalize automatically. Finally, you still may need a certain level of psychotherapy or psychological interventions, but they go much easier because you don't have to fight against the dysfunctional interoceptive systems. For example, the patient may need a self-efficacy prescription that involves skills of how he/she can control her/his inner state of being. That gives a great sense of self-efficacy. The example is an excellent illustration of how finding meaning in life is essential. It is a compelling way to fight depression ultimately.

Sensory-based Anxiety Prescription

A similar story applies to anxiety. The difference is that instead of having too few sensations in distress, people often experience too many strange feelings. People always strive to balance out and heal the interoceptive system, and once the interoceptive system is recovered, all the cognitive or psychological issues become much more comfortable to resolve.

This is a big part of anxiety for many people. Once you learn to be in contact with your interoceptive system, once you learn not to catastrophize when you feel something weird, then the anxiety also subsides. To summarize, once you go through all the prescriptions of stage one, you will start feeling good within your body. You will experience substantially less pain intention. Your sympathetic nervous system will bound regularly; you will have less cortisol. Your HPA axis will be a downregulated sympathetic pass system. Your relaxation system will be opera related. You will feel a much better sleep, you will wake up much fresher, your anxiety will decrease substantially as well as the depression, and you will have more energy. These are the things that usually happen, and they comprise stage one.

Nutrition and Exercise

Stage two starts after step one, which focuses exclusively on healing the interoceptive system. Once the interoceptive system is in a reasonably stable and good condition, there comes a time to start changing nutrition and introducing exercise. The goal of stage two is to make sure that you get better nutrition and that you exercise more, and if you need to lose weight in terms of nutrition, you need to change your food habits in case you have poor food habits. You need food that will supply your body with sufficient nutrients. You need to avoid foods that maintain and perpetuate high blood pressure. Previous discussions show how consumption of sweets, candies, cakes, and a lot of carbs leads to an increase in blood sugar, and ultimately in the insulin spike that overstimulates your sympathetic nervous system, adjusting food habits and food consumption to assist in weight loss. Exercising each night is not just a matter of exercising two, three times a week. What is more important is to introduce movement and exercise every hour or every hour and a half, especially if you have a job that requires you to sit most of the day. The reason being is that you need to shift your physiology from being as sedentary physiology or exercise physiology-based prescription.

Exercise prescription will help you to lose weight, decrease blood pressure, and make you more resistant to stressors. This is a reasonably important factor, an essential resolve, and the benefits of exercise. It is what makes you more resilient to stressors. It makes you less reactive to stressors. For example, if you take two people, where one wants to exercise regularly, and the other doesn't exercise, if you applied the same kind of stressor, you will find that people who exercise tend to be less reactive.

By the end of stage two, you will notice that you will have more energy, be more stress-resistant, you will lose weight, you will experience a much better mood, much better sleep. You will feel much better within your own body. You will have less pain, less muscle tension. As a result, you will experience and feel much higher safety and pleasantness within your organization, which will support the relaxation of your nervous system. Your HBA and sympathetic nervous system will get even more downregulated and also healthier.

Social and psychological Prescriptions

Stage three focuses primarily on social and psychological prescriptions. As a reminder, step one focuses on healing your interoceptive system. In phase two, you continue to work on your interoceptive order because it's the pollination of the healthy function of your sympathetic nervous system and your HP access. In stage two, you started changing your diet and introducing exercise. Finally, in phase three, you already understand the importance of social and psychological prescriptions. Therefore, what is this stage all about?

There are many psychological and social skills and functionalities that are very specific to you. All of them cannot be described here. The purpose of this part is to give you a couple of examples. One example and the functionality that you will build up in stage three is a stress shield. You remember that in previous chapters, it was evident that stress happens on the outside and over-activation of the SNS while HBX occurs on the inside.

The main issue is how to prevent this stress from affecting your physiologies, from overstimulating your sympathetic nervous system. The first thing that you can do is to use parasympathetic prescription where you activate your parasympathetic nervous system, and you learn to enter a state of being very relaxed. It's a very calm state. Recall two situations in your life. In one case, assume you weren't on vacation, you've slept well, you've acquired more wealth, everything is okay. The relationships are right; your nervous system is relaxed. The second state is when something is hurting. You're in conflict with your spouse; you didn't sleep well, you're agitated. When you compare these two states, how do your external stressors impact your life?

It is from your experience probably that when your entire physiology is relaxed, then you're not as reactive to external stressors. On the other hand, when you're sleep-deprived, when you conflict, when something is not going well, you're much more likely to react. You are much more reactive. If you want to build up a shield around you that will protect you from the effects of stress, the first thing you need to do is to build a solid foundation so that your baseline level of operation of the nervous system remains very calm and relaxed. As quiet as the baseline.

It does not mean that when you are stressed, you say everything is right. Many people misuse this kind of positive psychology by trying to persuade them that they are excellent and relaxed when they're not okay. That leads to even greater overstimulation of the sympathetic nervous system when you're trying to ignore or suppress something. Adopt physiological means to down-regulate your sympathetic nervous system, upregulate your sympathetic nervous system to create that foundation of calmness. You can try specific exercises, exercise prescription to be more specific decreases your reactivity chief stressors to ensure you're not as responsive to the stressors. You will end up building up a good solid foundation of calmness.

Additionally, through the exercise prescription, you become even less reactive. There are specific psychological skills that you can learn that ultimately change your perception. You can also finally think about shifting to a different environment. Something that you frequently forget is that you have power in your hands to change your situation positively. Case in point, if you don't like living in a city, you can change your setting, and you can move to a village. This is actually what people do in most cases.

You can, in the same way, choose what kind of people you associate with. And by changing the environment, by placing yourself in a different context where, for example, people are less trustful, less aggressive, you can also decrease the stress load on your system. There are also different kinds of skills, where you can learn as it has already been discussed, to prevent catastrophizing. In a nutshell, when something is not going well, many people start to ruminate to think over and over and over again. What happened? You should stop that process, not to suppress that process, but to resolve it. All of these factors build a stress shield. Think of this as an immediate evil castle, a big wall that protects you from this trust is life.

Purpose in Life.

Prescription having a purpose in life is essential and plays an important part in ensuring proper management and prevention of hypertension. It downregulates your sympathetic nervous system. It downregulates the inflammatory processes, and it has a beneficial effect on cardiovascular health. A high number of psychologists and psychotherapists contributed to developing this field of how to find a purpose in your life. There is a complementary approach. There is also use of the psychotherapeutic and psychological methods, but it is essential to begin from your physiology. You need to listen to the inner body sensations that your physiology sends you to optimize its state. If you think about it, when you are hungry, it's a sign from your physiology that it needs something from the external environment, and the same applies to food, to water to when you get tired or lonely. Loneliness is a feeling. It's a particular inner sensation set generated and sent to you by your physiology to tell you that you actually need communication and contact or warm and authentic contact with another human being.

It's just like food- the vital thing to understand that you are very different from a stone. Have you ever thought, how is it that you are different from a stone? Well, the thing is that the stone, as long as you protect it from rain and water, can exist. Millions and millions and probably billions of years from now, you cannot even exist for three days without the environment existing. The air, the water, the food, the social communication. You need all of these things. The next question therefore is, how do you know which things you do want? Well, inside of you, you have pretty intelligent psychology that tells you what it is that you need to optimize physiologically. It does so by sending internal inner body sensations. Therefore, when you are lonely, you feel certain feelings, for example, in your chest, and you have this desire to go out and meet friends.

When you are tired, you have a different inner body sensation that tells you that you need to do something like exercise. It seems like you have a different sensation. The problem is that you suppress and ignore these sensations, and this is how you lose physiology, and to the signals it sends us. These sickness signals, as mentioned before, they are vast and critical because this is how our physiology maintains homeostasis and optimizes its state by controlling your behavior. That's a crucial point. When you learn to listen to the inner body sensations and follow these internal body sensations, then you have learned to satisfy your deepest needs of the physiological system. It creates a purposeful life and a meaningful life.

On the other hand, when you ignore and suppress all these signals of your physiology, you start questioning whether this life has any meaning whatsoever. You can observe this happening in many people in Europe. This is especially prevalent in women who have dedicated their lives to supporting their children and their husbands. Whenever a person invests most of their time and energy in helping others, and while ignoring their own needs, they gradually start losing their internal purpose and meaning of life. Then when the kids go to college, and God forbid something happens with the relationship, the person no longer has an internal meaning in life because of all the purpose and meaning the person has to the external factors to the kids or the husbands disappear. This is why you are rebuilding the purposefulness and the meaning of life.

Once you are making your ability to follow the signals, your physiology that is trying to optimize its state of being, then immediately, you have acquired the foundational physiological purpose in life and meaning purpose in life. On top of that foundation, you can build more intricate and complicated goals and meanings in life. All the higher levels are now much stable.

Safe connection Prescription

Having a warm and authentic supportive relationship helps you to create a deep sense of safety that is essential. That's how a healthy nervous system works. From earlier discussions, you remember how safe connection together with the safe body creates a safe environment for yourself. The safe body and tranquil body make you experience safety and pleasant sensations inside of your body by building your human connections by creating a link to other human beings in an authentic warm manner. That is healing for your sympathetic nervous system.

Here are some examples of recent research. Cure and love reduce pain and stress. Here's an experiment that scientists have done. They took a woman and her, husband, and they attached electrodes to the woman. Through that Electrode, they delivered painful shocks to the woman. In one condition, the husband was not holding the woman. In the second condition, the husband was holding her tightly. What they found out is that in this latter condition, when the husband was holding her hand, she experienced substantially less pain.

Moreover, it was not just her subjective perception of the woman, but the brain areas and those that create a sense of pain that's registered as a sensor. They were activated less when the husband was holding his wife. The warmer and more authentic their relationship was the least pain felt and, on the other hand, more problematic, more conflicts they had and less friendly and genuine and supportive their relationship was, the less safe the link was, the more pain, the woman experienced. The two couples had this problematic relationship, and they put them through a special kind of couple therapy called emotionally focused therapy. They found out that when they compare the reduction in pain due to holding the hand by the husband before the treatment and after the treatment, the lesser the pain experienced by the woman. Thanks to her husband holding her hand after the procedure. That means that even if you have issues in your relationship and the relationship is not very warm and supportive; there is a good chance that you can actually go through the therapy and substantially improve the relationship. Research shows that this kind of treatment is useful for 70 to 80% in most bonds.

Why is it that the support and love and care are also important for your physiology and your health? The current understanding is that what psychologists and scientists called safe attachment is essential for your health and wellbeing. Initially, it was reasonably well established that this safe kind of attachment was significant for kids. There's a still face experiment by Dr Edward Tronic. It demonstrates the importance of a reliable emotional connection between the mother and the child. The same thing applies to adults. Even in childhood, the baby or the child needs that safe connection with the mother figure or the father figure, and when they grow up, they still need that kind of secure attachment.

Instead of having that face attachment, adults have a safe attachment with a partner. The current thinking is that this secure emotional supportive attachment is so evolutionary essential for you too. It's so critical that when you feel that you may lose this attachment, you get terrified. It's almost like you think that you will never have access to water again, never have access to food yet. That safe attachment is as important to you as to food and water, and therefore when you feel from your partner that you might be losing that secure attachment, you get scared. When you get terrified deep inside, you have different ways to express that fear. Some people express it as anger; some people collapse and retract from the context. There are tons of ways through which people express that fear, but no matter how they externally express that fear, it's vital to remember that you are fearful of losing that safe connection.

In another example, instead of a conversation between an adult and a child, this is a communication between two adults, two partners. One may say. "Oh God. Something is not working here." This is a demonstration of what happens often between the couples when this kind of safe connection, safe attachment is not there. The lack of safe attachment causes this kind of stress. It affects detrimentally on the health of both partners, especially when one of the partners has high blood pressure or any other type of cardiovascular condition. It is, therefore, crucial to restore safety and connection in your relationship.

The beauty of safety is that once you learn to create security inside of your body, inside of your physiology, and once you establish safe connections, you'll have a fantastic environment of safety that is very beneficial to your health.

Quality of life Prescription

Numerous factors create a deep state of wellbeing. Most of these factors have been discussed. These factors that create a deep sense of wellbeing, not only down-regulate your sympathetic nervous system, but they also provide a protective barrier from acquiring multiple medical, psychological, and mental health issues.

Shared Decision Making

Various studies provide evidence supporting the importance of multidrug therapy in reducing blood pressure for patients with hypertension and specific prevention organs in the body. However, this therapy has been proved to be aggressive as it should be. The total number of hypertensive patients in the 3rd world and developed nations with lowered blood pressure according to the national and international guidelines are still low and not encouraging.

Existing antihypertensive drugs are partially valid and partially ineffective. The reasons are likely to be due to difficulty in identifying symptoms in hypertension, dangers of the drugs' effects, and the desire for long-lasting treatment of hypertension.

Many patients are still of the belief that taking the drug for a short time can help heal the condition permanently. This may somehow be logical from a particular viewpoint —but is unethical. A well-tested approach to handling this issue is shared decision making (SDM). Shared decision-Making works differently as compared to the authoritarian tactic of physicians towards patients. According to the journal of Clinical hypertension, it is the act of involving patients in making medical choices thereby making the patient feel the independence and consent administration.

According to research conducted on shared decision making, it was discovered that patient empowerment through education programs directed towards various groups improves blood pressure control when combined with antihypertensive drug treatment. However, Mutual Decision Making applied in the hypertension management recorded minimal extra blood pressure reducing effects when compared to the education program.

That is due to two reasons; Foremost, from the onset, the SDM group showed much interest in this model than the control group. This was expected since the patients knew their groups from the initial of the study. Additionally, from both groups, there was an increase in SDM; the level was higher in the SDM group after 12 months as compared to the control patients.

Second, it was clear that having foundational know-how on the basics of hypertension was essentially sophisticated in the control group than in the other group. This was expected since having background knowledge added with a useful application of SDM would provide a better environment for control of blood pressure in the SDM group.

Results from the study indicate that better knowledge regarding hypertension and the planned readjustment of the decision-making process is effective in changing the affected peoples' behavior and attitudes on hypertension. Education programs play a critical role in the empowerment of patients.

Management of Hypertension in Rural Settings

Factors for effective hypertension management in a rural setting.

In modern society, hypertension is a new concept for local healthcare practitioners and local people. Most rural communities are only aware of traditional killer infections. From most rural communities in developing countries, it is clear that convenient infrastructure (dynamic and operative procedures of the local health professionals), deep awareness of causes of circulatory diseases in the local community and participative community are essential factors for effective implementation and sustainability hypertension program in local settings.

By applying upward and backward techniques, rural folks tend to join and expansively recognize the hypertension management program actively. Attracting the local community entirely is essential for developing new social levels for a healthy atmosphere to increase the will of the local people in countering hypertension or other cardiovascular diseases, risk factor prevention and assuring long-lasting sustainability.

According to the BMC Public Health journal, for a useful community hypertensive approach, a three dimensions' conceptual framework for circulatory diseases inhibition in public health should be integrated. This approach should incorporate an intervention strategy covering behavioral risk factors such as IEC efforts to minimize BP at society level by changes in behavioral risk factors, and development of functioning strategies for the high-risk group such as efforts to control BP in hypertensive using multiple drugs, exhausting the effect in primary care system to conduct health education promotions to population, screening and hypertension management.

That motivation is enough to initiate a hypertension management program without involving local administration or development of infrastructure suiting the course, such as a cardiac care staff at local health institutions. In communities that depict difficulty in absorbing and adopting new ideas, firm support, apparent contributions, and live examples from local administration can have a significant effect on the implementation of hypertension program, more so motivating shifts in the behavior, knowledge, and attitude of the whole population.

To build up a practical local cardiac care team training and support by the professional team is necessary. Standardized workflows to enable staff to minimize accidental errors or any new heavy burden of paperwork is also very essential. Cooperation between the local healthcare team and the deeply engaged local team in the program will also help in gaining enough confidence for future practice.

Factors affecting the adoption of local Diabetes Management Approaches
The two significant factors affecting the adoption of local level hypertension management programs are the severity of hypertension. How effective the hypertension treatment plan is. These two factors influenced how people decided on whether to adopt or walk away from the program.

People with hypertension will have to consider short term advantages of prevention and the disadvantages coming from regular checkups. Symptoms of hypertension majorly occur in the final stages. Many people do ignore these signs in earlier stages due to a lack of awareness of hypertension and other cardiovascular disease risk factors.

In reality, it is challenging for a working person to take most of their time for regular checkups. Having more than a few behavioral risk factors or past history of hereditary diseases are some of the factors inhibiting local populations from adopting the program. Just like in most developed countries, the high rate of hypertension is higher in women than in men, but this notion is reversed in some particular groups such as poor women, existing in the low economic end.

Prevention of Hypertension

As explained earlier, much of high blood pressure affliction or effect is felt by individuals not identified as hypertensive. For grassroots inhibition of hypertension: adults should ensure that their weight is sustainable and average, minimize consumption of salt while eating, avoid too much drinking of alcohol and sodas, exercise regularly and be on the move among other practices.

Chapter 11- FAQs

1. How best can hypertension be defined?

According to WHO, blood pressure is the force generated by the blood flowing against the arterial walls. Hypertension is, therefore, a condition when the blood pressure is extraordinary.

Blood pressure is recorded with two figures. The initial figure signifies systolic-blood vessel pressure during heart contraction. The final figure, diastolic- blood pressure in the blood vessels when the heart relaxes during heartbeats.

Hypertension is determined when both systolic pressure figure and diastolic pressure figure are measured in two days and the systolic blood pressure is above or equivalent to 140mmHg while the diastolic measurement be above or equivalent to 90 mmHg.

2. What are the significant hypertensive risk factors?

The most common risk factors are once described above. Changeable factors include unhealthy diets comprising excess salts, more fats, and trans fats, low fruit intake, low vegetable intake, inactive life, too much smoking, too much alcohol consumption, and being overweight.

Non-changeable risk factors include; above 65 years, family line with hypertension, kidney diseases, and diabetes.

3. How is obesity relating to Hypertension?

This is something that has been said all along both by health professionals and non-health professionals. According to Hillel Sternlicht and George L. Bakris, in their book *Primary hypertension*, this relationship has remained popular since the Framingham Heart Study. Nevertheless, the leading cause was not clear since adipose tissue was a hormonally and metabolically inert substance. More contemporary studies show the direct role played by visceral obesity in the development stabilization of hypertension. This journey is championed by an increase in the level of insulin and aldosterone. Leptin is manufactured and concealed by adipocytes; it regulates the sympathetic activity. Visceral fat also plays a role in the production of angiotensin, which is a substrate in the renin-angiotensin-aldosterone system. It leads to increased circulatory levels of aldosterone. Increased circulatory levels of aldosterone and enhanced sympathetic activity rise urinary sodium retention, thereby leading to hypertension. Obesity also overwhelms adiponectin secretion.

4. What are the popular signs of hypertension?

Hypertension is a dangerous condition and the leading cause of most deaths. It is a silent killer in that most individuals who have these conditions are unaware due to a lack of knowledge of its signs and symptoms. To avoid this, ensure you measure your blood pressure regularly.

Significant widespread symptoms include; morning headaches, continuous nose bleeding, irregular heartbeats, change in visions, and ear buzzes. Complicated hypertension causes general fatigue, vomiting, anxiety, pain in the chest, and pain in deep muscles.

The best way to identify whether one has hypertension or not is by consulting a very experienced doctor for useful measurement of blood pressure. The process is fast and unproblematic. You can also determine your blood pressure at home by adopting provided gadgets but ensure you consult a professional for more advice.

5. What do other Non-pharmacologic interventions help in the reduction of Blood Pressure?

Physical activity- intervention under physical activity includes aerobic, which reduces heart rate by 65-75 percent. It should be applied for a period of 90 to 150 minutes in 1 week. Dynamic resistance is also applicable. It also requires 60-150 minutes in a week and with 3- 6 exercises. Isometric strength-this should be conducted in 3 sessions and involves handgrips and rest between tasks. It should be done for 8 to 10 weeks.

Healthy diet- under a healthy diet, one needs to follow a DASH dietary pattern. The diet requires fruits, vegetables, whole grains, and low-fat dairy products that have a low level of saturated and total fat.

Weight loss- you should aim to reduce body fat. Lowering weight or fat should be the primary goal. Aim at reducing a minimum of 1 kg of the body weight and let it be the starting point.

Lowered consumption of dietary sodium- you should aim at 1500 mg in a day, but even 1000 mg can be a good starting point.

Increased intake of dietary potassium- you should consume 3000 mg to 5000 mg in a single day to stay on track. Consume a diet with lots of potassium.

Reduced alcohol consumption- if it is challenging to stop alcohol completely, men should reduce alcohol consumption to 2 drinks daily while women should take in 1 bottle daily.

6. What happens when Hypertension is not controlled?

Hypertension is very dangerous to a human heart when not controlled. When the pressure is high, the arteries may become hard, thereby decreasing the capacity of blood flowing to the heart. Oxygen flow to the heart is also reduced. In most cases, it results in occurrence of chest pains, and heart complications when the heart stops to circulate required blood level and oxygen to all parts of the body, inconsistent heartbeats that are considered death traps. heart attack- occurring when blood circulation to the heart is affected thereby leading to the death of heart muscles due to shortage of oxygen.

7. When can secondary causes of hypertension occur? And how can they be assessed?

Assessment of secondary causes of hypertension can be started depending on past history, physical examination, tests from the laboratory, or clinical suspicion. Someone with persistent hypokalemia is a prime suspect of secondary hypertension patients. Primary hyperaldosteronism is what majorly causes secondary hypertension. It can also be referred to as bilateral adrenal hyperplasia. It is not that all patients have hypokalemia; low normal potassium levels can also cause it.

Hypercortisolism (Cushing's syndrome or disease) is also considered as another form of secondary hypertension and majorly occurs in females. It comes in the form of central obesity and is different from obesity. Chemically, it can be related to hypokalemia and metabolic alkalosis. Many people confuse it with primary aldosteronism until one's level of aldosterone and cortisol becomes recognized.

Pheochromocytomas are also another form of secondary hypertension that is very unpopular. Related adrenal masses are usually recorded during a tomography scan. However, few of them have biochemical evidence indicating the prevalence of pheochromocytoma. Medical symptoms of pheochromocytomas include orthostatic hypotension, poor sleep quality. In most cases are they are found in a person's history. Some other symptoms include midnight wakeups with very high pressures and too many sweats.

8. What is the impact of dietary salt restriction in control of high blood pressure?

Sensitivity to salt is the impact of table salt consumption on Blood pressure. Rise in dietary salt leads to increased early and equal expansion of extracellular fluid volume and increased cardiac output. To cover for the hemodynamic changes and to maintain stable blood pressure with high consumption of sodium, peripheral vascular resistance reduces, and this is related to increased manufacture of nitric oxide. Among the slat sensitive people, reduction in peripheral vascular resistance and the increase in nitric oxide are impaired or absent in salt sensitivity, leading to increased blood pressure in such individuals.

9. Why is hypertension highly prevalent in 3rd world countries?

According to the World Health Organization, the rebalance of heart attacks depends on the regions' income group. WHO states that Africa has the highest occurrence rate of 27% compared to America, which has an 18% prevalence.

Recent research showed an increase in the number of adults with hypertension from 5944 million in 1975 to approximately 1 billion in 2015. Most increases were recorded in developing countries. This is due to a rise in hypertension risk factors in these countries.

10.   Why are the renin-angiotensin system blockers favored for diabetic nephropathy patients?

ACE inhibitors and ARBs are generally considered for antihypertensive therapy for people with diabetes. They slow down the development of chronic kidney disease (CKD)

Compared to other drugs in spite of related reductions in blood pressure. Research from patients with Stage 3 and 4 chronic kidney disease checking how these agents react to both type 1 and type 2 diabetes indicated superior reduction compared to conventional blood pressure-lowering therapy. Even though there is a little more evidence for ARB than ACE inhibitor therapies, their effectiveness is related to an equal reaction. It, therefore, means that all agents have the same therapeutic efficacy.

11. Why are thiazide-type diuretics considered the best agents for the early stages of hypertension?

From all existing antihypertensive agents in the clinical field, thiazide-type diuretics are the famous, prolonged standing, widely used, registering a steady reduction in morbidity and mortality in all groups of people tried. Even though low-dose hydrochlorothiazide (HCTZ) is widely prescribed for patients by various physicians, contemporary research shows that a higher dosage of hydrochlorothiazide (HCTZ) has massive positive impacts on the management of blood pressure. Furthermore, considering the influence of sodium on hypertension, more so in the elderly African population who are salt sensitive, natriuresis agents play a very significant role.

12. What really causes primary hypertension?

The cause and development of primary hypertension are complicated and research on this field is very limited. Primary hypertension is inherited; it is evident that various ecological and inherited factors combine for its development. Blood pressure comes by due to the impact of systemic vascular resistance and cardiac output; it actively develops when the systemic vascular resistance becomes stronger. Various researches have shown a connection in the kidney, vasculature, central and SNS, immune system, and cardiovascular system to the formation and maintenance of systemic hypertension. An increase in body sodium and over-activation of the renin-angiotensin-aldosterone axis, among others, are the primary cause of higher blood pressure.

13. What are the popular negative effects of antihypertensive drugs?

Physicians need to inform their patients of the adverse effects of these drugs to avoid future complains from the patients. Even though these effects are common, they do not apply to all patients.

- ϑ Blockage in the urinary tract
- ϑ orthostatic hypotension
- ϑ bronchospasm, weight gain and in some cases, they cause erectile dysfunction though this has not been confirmed
- ϑ Lower extremity oedema, gingival hyperplasia, fever, massive headaches, and change in skin appearance
- ϑ Inconsistent coughs, angioedema (more research being done), and hyperkalemia
- ϑ impaired glucose tolerance, photosensitivity, body rash, and orthostatic hypotension

14. What is the immediate therapy for hypertension?

Immediate therapy depends on age, how the kidney functions, body reactions, and ethnicity. As discussed in earlier chapters, common and more comfortable causes of hypertension that are easy to treat, like diet, patterns of sleep, and medications should be considered in the first place. After that, in the case of patients with stage I hypertension, monotherapy using calcium channel blocker, thiazide-like diuretic, or renin-angiotensin system blocker can be considered as fists therapies.

For diabetic and heart failure patients, considering ACEi iARB therapy would do wonders. b-blockers are not preferred for Blood pressure-lowering therapy but are essential for those with heart failure.

15. Is self-blood pressure measuring effective?

Measuring and monitoring blood pressure privately or in the ambulance is useful in determining whether there is a problem in the cardiovascular system as compared to office measurements. Research has shown that the self-blood pressure test ensures control of blood pressure and adherence to medications. This technique identifies hidden cases and symptoms of blood pressure; BP readings when one is feeling sleepy is essential to determining the status of blood pressure.

Wrist-based cuff devices may not be that reliable. It would be best if you instead went for the upper arm. Even though many units, it is challenging to validate and prove the results. In this case, well-tested machines should be purchased. The best-tested method is the use of oscillatory measurements. Mechanisms should be well taken care of regularly.

16. What is the current Hypertension prevalence worldwide?

The prevalence of hypertension increases according to age. Individuals who are 80 years old are 90% more likely to have hypertension. According to world health organizations, an estimated 1.13 billion individuals in the whole world have hypertension. About 2/3 of this population are living in both developed and 3rd world countries.

According to the 2015 survey by WHO, 1 in 4 men and 1 in 5 women were hypertensive. Less than 1 in 5 people have their hypertension conditions being taken care of. It is the primary cause of early deaths globally. According to the baseline survey of 2010, a target on no communicable diseases has been set to reduce hypertension prevalence by 25% by 2025. In America, hypertension is shared among the African American population.

17. What is the best solution for hypertension?

By preventing hypertension, you are avoiding the possibility of heart attack., kidney problems, and stroke, which are the major killer diseases.

To prevent hypertension;

- ◄ Reduce trans fats in your daily diets
- ◄ Reduce saturated fat foods
- ◄ Stay away from tobacco
- ◄ Avoid alcohol by any means
- ◄ Exercise regularly to remain physically active
- ◄ Consume more fruits
- ◄ Consume more vegetables
- ◄ Reduce salt intake. Take a maximum of 5 grams daily.

To manage hypertension;

- ◄ Ensure you treat high blood pressure
- ◄ Regularly check your blood pressure
- ◄ Effectively manage metal stress
- ◄ Manage to exit medical conditions effectively.

According to the International Society of hypertension, the following are the most frequently asked questions;

18. In case you have blood pressure and are thinking of getting pregnant, is it wise to consult a doctor first?

In case you have high blood pressure and are considering getting pregnant, ensure you consult a health professional for further advice. This is due to the fact that high blood pressure always brings pregnancy complications for the fetus and the mother.

Blood pressure can be treated during pregnancy, but only certain drugs can be used, and your doctor knows which drugs are safe and which should be avoided.

After the age of eighteen, people should speak to their doctor about blood pressure and ask for a reading every two years. The blood pressure reading should be taken from both arms to note any differences. Remember that history of high blood pressure warrants more frequent readings.

Furthermore, occasional health resource fairs or other community organizations will have blood pressure screenings. Make sure to monitor levels as often as possible,

regardless of the regularity of your doctor visits.

Note that one hour before the test, people shouldn't drink coffee or smoke any tobacco products to keep blood pressure rates regular. Furthermore, people should sit still for at least five minutes before the test because blood pressure can elevate when moving around.

19. Are diabetics required to be more careful with their blood pressure as compared to other populations?

Diabetes is a very sensitive condition in the human body that must be taken care of. Diabetes increases the possibility of contracting cardiovascular diseases and blood pressure.

Generally, it is advisable to treat blood pressure in lower level diabetics compared to nondiabetic individuals.

20.   Is high blood pressure cured?

It is incurable but controllable. Curing and controlling are two confusing words that must be looked at deeply. Contemporary therapeutic methodologies to blood pressure exist in plenty and are secure. Nevertheless, when one stops treatment, high blood pressure tends to return at a faster rate. Once you start a hypertension plan, you should not stop. There are testimonies of people who have lost their lives after braking from the hypertension treatment plan. Some people have been admitted to Intensive Care Units by taking for granted simple directions from their health professionals. By accepting the fact that hypertension cannot be cured, you need to change your attitude, organize, lace-up, and change your lifestyle. You will not die when you heed to available tested advice from health experts. In fact, research has it that you can stay longer than individuals with normal blood pressure when you effectively follow the hypertension management plan

21. Why should prehypertension be treated?

Individuals having prehypertension but no primary arterial complications can be handled with Blood pressure-reducing drugs. People with prehypertension are more likely to die and have a higher chance of contracting cardiovascular complications compared to those whose blood pressure value is below 120 mmHg. Current clinical studies have provided more information indicating the benefit of reducing systolic BP from 140 mmHg to under 130 mmHg.

Besides high blood pressure being a major cause of cardiovascular disease, prehypertension has some additional risks on top of the popular risk for cardiovascular disease: the growth of hypertension and negative impact on related body parts. In a group study conducted in Porto Alegre, Brazil, 4/5 of individuals with prehypertension contacted hypertension within a decade. Such cases have been experienced among other populations, like in the case of a national section of Japanese workers.

Damage to dependent organs of individuals having prehypertension has been depicted in many studies. Case in point, in the Checking of patterns and Factors in Cardiovascular Disease (MONICA) group, prehypertensive people at the starting point who still had prehypertension during the regular evaluation period had high chances of developing increased mass of the left ventricle when compared to individuals who had ordinary blood pressure.

According to study statistics from the Atherosclerosis Risk in Communities (ARIC), prehypertension has a relation with irregularities in cardiac arrangement and function in grown-ups.

Two clinical studies conducted among hypertensive individuals have shown the effect of antihypertensive treatment in lowering the influence of hypertension in individuals with systolic BP in the range of (130 -140 mmHg). In an Experimental study on Prevention of Hypertension, hypertension prevalence more than two years was inhibited in approximately 67% of individuals administered with a typical medication of candesartan. This advantage declined when the treatment was stopped. In a study on Inhibition of Hypertension using Angiotensin-Converting Enzyme Inhibitor Ramipril in high blood pressure individuals, ramipril reduced the possibility of hypertension by approximately 35%.

22. Where can one contact for more information?

No one else apart from your doctor. Your doctor has the best information pertaining to your health.

23. How prevalent is high blood pressure?

In most cases, around 4 in 10 adults who are over 25 years have hypertension, and in other regions, another 1 in 5 suffer from prehypertension. Research has it that the majority of people who reach the age of 80 have higher chances of developing hypertension. About ½ of blood pressure-related complications is prevalent in individuals with high-pressure levels.

24. Why is it essential to measure blood pressure?

Knowing your blood pressure is very important in that it is the force that drives blood from the heart to the lungs and then to all other parts of the body.

However, it is very important to understand your blood pressure. In most cases, it results in increased exposure to critical heart diseases, such as heart attack, stroke, kidney complications, and visual blurriness.

Conclusion

The intensification of obesity results in a rise in hypertension. There is a direct relation between the two. When the occurrence of hypertension increases, resistant hypertension also increases. From various research, it is evident that the use of ACE inhibitors, ARBs, calcium antagonists, and thiazide diuretics in treating hypertension has some positive impact. However, there are more emerging strategies that can be adopted to manage hypertension.

When treating patients with hypertension in the hospital, the main aim is to develop and apply appropriate precautionary and therapeutic strategies fitting the patient's physical and emotional ability to adhere.

From reading this book, it is a fact that you have a solid understanding of blood pressure, how to manage your blood pressure without using drugs. You are on the right path to a healthy and long-lasting life.

The most important advice you need is that every step you make in life counts. Celebrate every achievement you make in life in relation to weight loss. Take daily, small steps to ensure consistency and sustainability. Always be optimistic, be focused, set your goal, be determined. Remember that your life matters.

Way Forward

From the discussions above, it is clear that efficient modern research has increased the people's knowledge about various ways nurses adopt in the promotion of health. Explanation as to why hypertension has increased is also well laid out. However, general knowledge is not yet clear. More research should still be carried out on the subject with deep data collection and analysis procedures.

Primarily, health care professionals such as the nurses, pharmacists, midwives, doctors, social workers, among others, are the people with a firsthand idea on the subject. This is a good gesture since the information gained can be trusted. Healthcare professionals are trustworthy when it comes to medical advice. Health care workers must, therefore, exploit that opportunity completely. Creating public awareness on immediate prevention of high blood pressure should be the number one objective. Making people aware of possible lifestyle changes should be put into consideration. Such awareness leads to self-empowerment and an individual feeling that every person is the sole caretaker of their health.

Health professionals should explain readings from blood pressure measurements. This will promote public awareness of consistent blood pressure interpretations. It will also lead to increased knowledge since disparity in measurement can be evaluated independently.

Both local and urban health campaigns on the dangers of too much salt should be initiated. This strategy is affordable and has a prolonged positive outcome on the general health standard of the population. Educating the community, more so women will positively impact the societal, national and family health. This is because the African culture considers the woman as a leader in the kitchen.

It is very important to understand the ABC of high blood pressure. Health care workers must also address the high debate on potential dangers of this condition as one of the leading grounds of HBP. Understanding that risky lifestyle behaviors such as excessive consumption of alcohol, excessive consumption of salt, inactive lifestyle- with less exercise, continuous smoking, and unbalanced nutrition are the leading factors for high blood pressure despite the existence of other chronic factors. Training and awareness creation on positive lifestyle should be the key point for public health professionals.

Classified Hypertension Information
Use juices to maintain a healthy heart.

Juicing is an essential art of marinating a healthy heart. Juicing makes good use of ripe fruits. Below are recipes for effective juicing; however, it is necessary to note that they cannot be considered first when the DASH diet is available. It is also not a recommendation for juice fasting. When you have made up your mind to do juice fasting, always ensure you inform your doctor for more advice. You will need a blender to be successful.

Coleman et al. provides the following juicing recipe;

breakfast

- 1 cup of frozen mixed berries
- One medium banana
- One medium pear
- 2 ounces frozen orange juice concentrate
- 4 oz. egg substitute
- 8. nonfat or low-fat milk or almond milk
- 8. water or orange juice

Summer Medley

- 2 cups cantaloupe melon chunks
- 2 cups honeydew melon chunks
- 2 cups seedless watermelon chunks
- Two tablespoons honey
- 8 oz. orange juice

Strawberry-Banana Smoothie with Cocoa

- One medium banana
- One scoop Profibe
- 2 cups fresh or frozen strawberries
- 2 oz. frozen white grape juice
- Two tablespoons cocoa powder
- 4 oz. egg substitute
- 8 oz. nonfat or low-fat milk or almond milk
- 8 oz. water

Recipe for healthy blood pressure
Sweet Potato Salad

- Salt (optional)
- Low-fat mayonnaise
- 1/3 cup walnuts, chopped
- Two tablespoons lemon juice
- Two large sweet potatoes with skin
- 1 cup celery (4 to 5stalks), diced

Creamy vegetable soup

- 1 cup low-fat sour cream
- ½ teaspoon ground white pepper
- ½ teaspoon tarragon
- ½ teaspoon thyme

Avocado soup

- Recipe Makes 4 Servings.
- Nutrition Information per Serving:
- Calories:80
- Sodium: 50 mg
- Carbohydrates: 8g
- Fat: 5 g

- Protein: 2 g

Tomato extract is also good. According to a research carried out on a small group of people, individuals with stage 1 high blood pressure, took 250 milligrams of tomato extract containing 15 milligrams of lycopene daily for eight weeks. Daily intake of tomato extract led to a drop in systolic blood pressure by ten drops and four drops in diastolic blood pressure.

Good diet plays an integral role in the management and treatment of hypertension. Well, it is not possible to list all food in that category, but it is important to note that you must not restrict yourself to the recipes mentioned above. There are lots of books, blogs, and information all over the internet that provides more recipe that will help you handle your blood pressure. Above all, consult your doctor to determine how you will react to the recipe and the advantages. Hypertension is dangerous, but it can be effectively managed when we independently make wise decisions on our health. The only secret involves regular exercise, eating a healthy diet as described above, minimize alcohol, minimize sodas, minimize smoking if you cannot stop it, have a positive attitude, be perceptible to change, set objectives which will then make you achieve your desired goal, consider losing weight if your weight is high.

Useful resources

Implementing a hypertension management program in a rural area. Available at http://www.biomedcentral.com/1471-2458/11/325

importance of physical activity. Available at,

http://medicdictionary.thefreedictionary.com/exercise

NICE guidelines in 2010. Hypertension in pregnancy: diagnosis and management.
http://nice.org.uk/guidance/cg107

Journal of American hypertension.
https://doi.org/10.1016/j.jash.2018.01.004

New Concepts and Recommendations, Pharmacological Research (2018), https://doi.org/10.1016/j.phrs.2018.10.001

Low blood pressure system. Available at www.express.co.uk

Ultimate Testo explosion. available at
https://weightlosstop.com

Huntingtonnews. Available at www.huntingtonnews.com

CPSIA information can be obtained
at www.ICGtesting.com
Printed in the USA
LVHW041355261020
669802LV00002BA/471

9 781801 091978